SYNERGY

Synergy

THE ESSENCE OF MARRIAGE

Ibukun Adewusi

CCCG Publishing House

Contents

Author: Ibukun Adewusi

ISBN: 978-1-989099-24-7 (hardcover)
ISBN: 978-1-989099-25-4 (ebook)

First Printing 2023

Dedication

To the Holy Spirit (HS), thank you for being my friend, partner, and teacher on this journey of establishing and maintaining synergy in my marriage. Thank you for the corrections, revelations, and love you keep showing me. Thank you for the strength and grace you gave me in writing this book. I love you HS!

To my lovely husband, Emmanuel Adewusi, thank you for your amazing support, covering, words of encouragement, direction, and prayers as I ventured into writing this book. Thank you for being such an understanding and patient husband, as God continues to mold and fuse us together as one according to His perfect design and will. I'm truly blessed to have you on my side as we journey this life together and pursue God's vision for our lives and marriage.

Foreword

"Therefore shall a man leave his father and his mother, and shall cleave unto his wife: and they shall become one flesh." (Genesis 2:24, NKJV)

Marriage is a sacred vow between a man and woman, to "become one flesh which was instituted by God. The concept of 'Marriage', with the focus, specifically on how to have the perfect union, has been the topic of discussion for many years, with the aim to identify what is needed to make a marriage work. Many books on marriage have been written, focusing on the different ingredients that make a successful marriage, such as communication, commitment, finance, lovemaking, the God-factor, and many more. These topics have also extended to counseling sessions, webinars, and even couple's seminars. Nevertheless, with the many books, guidelines, and resources out there, why are there still failed marriages?

According to statistics, there were approximately 2.7 per 1,000 people that got divorced in America in 2021. This means that there are around 750,000 divorces per year in America. That is an alarming number! The most shocking aspect though, is that these divorces cut across all categories of people, irrespective of their color, faith, social status, or years of experience. Else who would have imagined that the likes of Bill Gates, and Jeff Bezos would go through a divorce with their experience as entrepreneurs and the conglomerates that they control? So, it got me wondering how these known names are able to control a conglomerate and yet a seemingly small unit as their marriage failed.

This confirms that marriage goes beyond the technical know-how of successful business leaders. The reason for a divorce is usually summed up as "irreconcilable differences" - which usually stem from lack of trust, communication, disagreement on finances, and sometimes abuse. Some marriages have also become a competition arena where couples cleave to themselves and not their spouses. But now, having read this book, I would term these irreconcilable differences as a lack of synergy.

This book, 'Synergy: The Essence of Marriage,' which according to the author, was inspired by the Holy Spirit, is very impactful and insightful. Synergy is defined as the interaction of elements, that when combined, produce a total effect that is greater than the sum of the individual element's contribution. Deuteronomy 32:30 says, "*How could one chase a thousand, and two put ten thousand to flight..*" In this book, the act of grafting is used as an apt illustration to describe synergy in marriage. Grafting is the act of placing a portion of one plant (bud, scion) into a stem root or branch of another stock in such a way that a union is formed, and the partners will continue to grow. Similarly, in the context of marriage, a man will leave his father and mother and be joined to his wife, and they become one flesh and continue to grow. The author further explained how the synergy can be maintained in marriage through spiritual authority which is in three folds: the Word, the Holy Spirit, and the human authorities. Therefore, a man and his wife need spiritual authority in order to have synergy in finance, body, physical appearance, and feelings.

Pastor Ibukun Adewusi is a wife, pastor, writer, a role model who has used her ministry to impact and bring restoration and transformation to families; which she believes is the bedrock of any nation. As the popular saying goes, "charity begins at home". As I read each chapter of this book,' I took account of my own marriage and started checking off the things that have kept the synergy alive in my marriage, and was also reminded of the areas where I have relaxed that need to be revived. This book is a must-read if you are seeking synergy in your marriage or if you are wanting to be reminded of how to keep or revive the synergy in your marriage.

By: Pastor Mike Olawale

Lead Pastor, Christ Dominion Church of God International

Introduction

From a very young age, I have always been enamoured with "love" (relationships) or anything relating to it. This led to the one burning question that I would ask anyone I possibly could: "How would you know the right person to get married to?" I almost always left frustrated since most of the responses to this question were "You will just know." It seemed like such a vague answer. As time went on, I started looking for answers in romantic movies, which I discovered were fictional; but with time, my question metamorphosed into a burning question of my soul to know "the essence of marriage." I knew marriage went beyond two good people coming together in holy matrimony, and I was even aware that it had to do with vision; however, I sincerely lacked the understanding of the essence of marriage. It was so crucial for me to find the right answer to this burning question of mine because I did not want to follow most people to say "marriage was good" and be satisfied with that. I truly yearned to understand and get the revelation of the essence and purpose of marriage. Dr. Myles Munroe once said, "When purpose is not known, abuse is inevitable," and if I was to slightly reword it in this context, "When purpose [of marriage] is not known, abuse is inevitable." After a long quest of discovery and revelation, if I were to summarize the essence of marriage in one word, it would be "**SYNERGY**."

1

The Foundation of Synergy

WHAT IS SYNERGY?

According to the Cambridge Dictionary, synergy is "the **combined power** of a group of things when they are **working together**, that is **greater than** the total power achieved by **each working separately**." My personal definition of synergy is "an effective and efficient team effort that produces results greater than the individuals combined." Let us look at Ecclesiastes 4:9-12 where a beautiful picture of synergy is painted for us.

"9 Two are better than one, because they have a good [more satisfying] reward for their labor; 10 For if they fall, the one will lift up his fellow. But woe to him who is alone when he falls and has not another to lift him up! 11 Again, if two lie down together, then they have warmth; but how can one be warm alone? 12 And though a man might prevail against him who is alone, two will withstand him. A threefold cord is not quickly broken." (AMPC)

In simple terms, synergy is the result of unity and oneness. It eliminates the "I" syndrome and introduces the "We" concept and can, therefore, never be achieved if division exists. It is no wonder there is a saying that goes, "No man is an island on his own." In life, there are three stages that we pass through:

1. **Dependent Stage** - This is commonly seen with babies who depend solely on their parents for food, clothing, and shelter.
2. **Independent Stage** - In this stage, they discover and explore who they are, their ideologies, strengths, and personal goals. Although we were created to grow beyond this stage into the final one, many people tend to stop at this one.
3. **Interdependent Stage** - At this stage, the goal is not to lose independence, but to instead realize that human beings were created to be interconnected and not what we know as a "lone wolf." Persons at this stage realize the strengths of others and leverage this to their benefit to produce a more fruitful result. This is the essence of synergy. It is understanding that none of us alone are as good as all of us combined.

Although the concept of synergy is highly sought after and can be seen in operation in many different settings, such as workplaces, communities, nations, etc., this book will zoom into its operation within the confines of marriage.

THE RIGHT FOUNDATION

Before a building is erected, it is essential for the foundation to be laid first, as this ultimately determines the building's strength. The choice of materials and their quality are also crucial for the foundation to stand the test of time and remain intact. Failure to consider this can result in defects, cracks, and tons of other negative outcomes. A foundation is normally built by pouring a mixture of cement, water, and sand. After these three components have been mixed and poured, they undergo a curing process that fuses them, resulting in a strong foundation. Now, can you imagine mixing oil, sand, and water instead? This would surely be a disaster waiting to happen. Even more so since oil and water naturally do not mix. But just how critical the materials of a foundation are, to build a strong and long-lasting building, the same principle applies in marriage.

Although God designed marriage to have a synergistic effect, for this to become a reality, the foundation of the marriage must be carefully constructed and cemented. The Bible tells us in 2 Corinthians 6:14-15 not to be unequally yoked with unbelievers, but have you ever wondered why? It is because a proper fusion can't occur when both parties have opposing principles, values, ideologies, and belief systems. When the ingredients that make up the core of one person are completely different from the other person, regardless of how hard they try to make it work, it ends up in friction and division. In the same way that we cannot mix oil and water, so is the case for a union between an unbeliever and a believer. This is why Amos 3:3 says, *"Can two walk together except they are agreed."* (NKJV)

Let us examine a passage that I came across in Daniel 2:41-43 that further depicts this truth:

" 41 And as you saw the feet and toes, partly of [baked] clay [of the potter] and partly of iron, it shall be a divided kingdom; but there shall be in it some of the firmness and strength of iron, just as you saw the iron mixed with miry [earthen] clay. 42 And as the toes of the feet were partly of iron and partly of [baked] clay [of the potter], so the kingdom shall be partly strong and partly brittle and broken. 43 And as you saw the iron mixed with miry and earthen clay, so they shall mingle themselves in the seed of men [in marriage bonds]; but they will not hold together [for two such elements or ideologies can never harmonize], even as iron does not mingle itself with clay." (AMPC)

In the above excerpt, as believers, we symbolize "iron" and un-believers as the "clay." Though the iron (believer) is strong by itself, the moment it joins itself (in marriage) with clay (an unbeliever), its strength is reduced. As a result, division and disunity set in, limiting the impact the union could have achieved if they were from the same spiritual kingdom. We see this unfold in the story of the tower of Babel, in Genesis 11:1-9, where they were united with one purpose and one language. When God saw what they were building, even He acknowledged that they would certainly achieve it; however, since their purpose was misaligned with His, He gave them different languages. This caused confusion and division, thus halting their mission. When a believer, who has sworn his/her allegiance to Jesus Christ, marries an unbeliever, who has no allegiance to Jesus Christ, the outcome can be akin to both parties speaking different languages. Communication and understanding cease, and instead of synergy, frustration eventually builds up. This is the reason why iron requires another iron to increase its strength and sharpness.

"As iron sharpens iron, so one person sharpens another." (Proverbs 27:17, NIV)

Ensuring your marriage is built on a solid foundation requires you to first give your life to Jesus Christ and allow Him to be your personal Lord and Saviour. This is the first step towards a journey of synergy. If you would like to make this decision today, please turn to the end of this book to repeat the Sinner's Prayer with me.

2

The Art of Grafting

"Therefore a man shall leave his father and mother and be joined to his wife, and they shall become one flesh." (Genesis 2:24, NKJV)

I was first introduced to the concept of grafting back in high school when my agricultural instructor presented this topic in one of the classes. I was fascinated by the fact that one part of a plant can be joined to another by tying them up, and they continue to grow together as one. It seemed like something from a fictional movie, but this time, it was real. This seemed like surgery on a plant which wowed me. Fast forward to many years later, in the middle of the night, the Holy Spirit woke me up and began reminding me of my encounter with the concept of grafting in high school and began to show me the link between grafting and marriage. I was blown away (I usually am when the Holy Spirit begins His teaching moments), and as I went into further research about grafting and exploring the different benefits it brings to both plants, I began to see the similarities with synergy in a marriage. Later, we will explore some of the benefits that emerge from grafting or synergy, but now, let's look at what grafting is all about.

WHAT IS GRAFTING?

According to the Encyclopedia Britannica, grafting is defined as "the act of placing a portion of one plant (bud or scion) into or on a stem, root or branch of another (stock) in such a way that a union will be formed and the partners will continue to grow. The part of the combination that provides the root is called the stock; the added piece is called the scion."

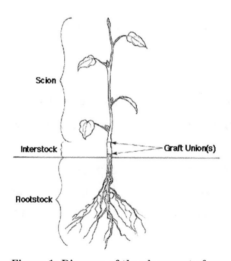

Figure 1: Diagram of the placement of an interstock in a grafting process
Bilderback, Ted, and R.E. Bir, and T.G.Ranney. "Grafting and Budding Nursery Crop Plants". Published June 30, 2014, at NC State Extension Publications, https://content.ces.ncsu.edu/ grafting-and-budding-nursery-crop-plants

In grafting, a detachment and a joining process occur before a union is formed. Likewise, in marriage, a detachment initially happens when the man leaves his father and mother (initial tree/family unit) and is then joined to his wife; whereby, the two become one flesh or union (new tree/family unit). This is the reason why some couples begin to look alike physically, think alike, finish each other's statements, and even experience similar emotions. I recall in the early years of our marriage, I was going through a challenge and was feeling discouraged. At the same time, my husband's enemy suddenly started feeling the same emotions. He rebuked it and was wondering where those emotions came from and by the inspiration from the Holy Spirit, got the revelation that it was from me experiencing those emotions. He reached out to me, and after receiving confirmation, he pondered why that happened. The Holy Spirit revealed to him that because we were now one as a couple, such things were bound to happen. In marriage, oneness is not just physical (sexual intercourse), but it is intended for a couple to experience oneness with their souls (will, mind, emotions) and spirits as well.

THE GRAFTING PROCESS

It is not enough to take parts of different plants and bring them together. You might be wondering, what would hold them together or prevent them from falling apart? The joining process in grafting is aided by a grafting tape or cord that helps with the binding process by tying both plants together to prevent either from slipping away from the other. As I continued exploring the concept of grafting in marriage with the Holy Spirit that night, I had several questions for Him, such as, "What symbolizes the cord in marriage?" But one particular one I had was, "Why did it say in Ecclesiastes 4:12 that *a threefold cord is not quickly [easily] broken?*" This statement in scripture puzzled me because I was under the impression that a threefold cord has greater strength and could NEVER be broken. I didn't understand why it said, "*not quickly [easily] broken,*" as that meant to me there was a "possibility" of breaking. I began asking the Holy Spirit questions, such as, "Why?" and "How?" and over time, He continued to give me more and more revelation. (Oh, how I love the teaching moments of the Holy Spirit.)

THE CORD IN MARRIAGE

To draw a more full and concise picture, let us take a look at a few of the verses that precede Ecclesiastes 4:12:

"8 This is the case of a man who is all alone, without a child or a brother, yet who works hard to gain as much wealth as he can. But then he asks himself, "Who am I working for? Why am I giving up so much pleasure now?" It is all so meaningless and depressing.9 Two people are better off than one, for they can help each other succeed. 10 If one person falls, the other can reach out and help. But someone who falls alone is in real trouble. 11 Likewise, two people lying close together can keep each other warm. But how can one be warm alone? 12 A person standing alone can be attacked and defeated, but two can stand back-to-back and conquer. Three are even better, for a triple-braided cord is not easily broken." (Ecclesiastes 4:8-12, NLT)

Verses 8-11 perfectly depict the concept of synergy by illustrating the power and benefits of two. This isn't just within the confines of marriage but can apply to any relationship, although for this book, we will concentrate on the aspect of marriage.

The cord (grafting cord) that binds a man and a woman together is love and it takes different forms. "The Four Loves" by C.S. Lewis explains how this love can take on these different forms:

1. **Affection (Storge)** - Commonly seen between a parent and child
2. **Friendship (Philia)** - Experienced between friends
3. **Romantic (Eros)** - Between lovers
4. **Charity (Agape)** - Unconditional love of God for mankind and also the greatest and purest love

The Holy Spirit further explained to me that a determining factor of a successful grafting process in marriage depends on how tight or loose the cord is woven around both plants. For example, gluing two items together, most adhesives suggest applying pressure to the items to ensure they are adequately fused. The same applies to marriage. Can you imagine having the cord loosely tied around the two plants? This would cause a gap between both plants and prolong the grafting period. Over time, if the cord remains untightened, one plant will eventually fall away from the other, thus halting the fusing process. This is why when love is loosely present in a marriage, detachment becomes inevitable, which can eventually lead to separation or even divorce if the bond remains loose. This is one of the underlying reasons why you might have heard some couples say they "fell out of love," stopped loving the other person, or are no longer in love with their spouse. Any love outside the love of Jesus is conditional and has the possibility of fading away when those conditions that attracted them to the other person are absent. A couple's love will stand the test of time when it is rooted in the love of Jesus. This is because God is love, and when their love for each other is embedded in the love of Jesus, it brings Him into the equation of their marriage, and He becomes the glue that binds them together because His love is the greatest and the strongest of love.

"We know how much God loves us, and we have put our trust in his love. God is love, and all who live in love live in God, and God lives in them." (1 John 4:16, NLT)

THE INTERSTOCK:
THE POWER OF THREE

"A person standing alone can be attacked and defeated, but two can stand back-to-back and conquer. Three are even better, for a triple-braided cord is not easily broken." (Ecclesiastes 4:12, NLT)

We've commonly heard that two is better than one, but did we just read that three is even better? Wow! When I first came across this scripture, it stirred up my curiosity, and I yearned to know who the third person could be. I did not want to settle for the 'good old two' but longed for the best option of three. The Holy Spirit later revealed that the third party is **Spiritual Authority**. This revelation excited me because He began to show me the benefits a marriage derives from being under the covering of spiritual authority, and how that helps to establish synergy in a marriage. Later, we will explore some of these benefits in more detail, but you may wonder, who or what is spiritual authority? In simple terms, a spiritual authority is someone or something you have given authority or permission to influence you. To learn more about the concept of spiritual authority, you can refer to the book, "*The Blessings of Being Under Spiritual Authority*" by Emmanuel Adewusi.

I was excited about this revelation of spiritual authority as the third party, but my excitement grew exponentially when I discovered that in the grafting process, there is something called an interstock or intermediate stock. An interstock is a piece of a tree trunk that is inserted between a rootstock and a scion to aid the union between incompatible varieties (Merriam-Webster Dictionary; Ted, Bilderback, et al.) This fascinated me because the Holy Spirit began to show me the similarity between an interstock and a spiritual authority. According to the Cambridge Dictionary, two plants can be "incompatible," meaning they are "unable to exist or work with another person or thing because of basic differences." Likewise in marriage, there are times when because of our uniqueness, without insight and proper understanding of the other person, it could be a challenge to dwell with the other person. And that is where spiritual authority comes in as the glue that keeps a husband and wife together as one.

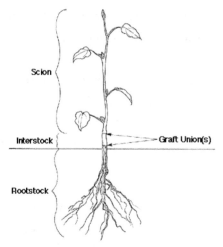

**Figure 1: Diagram of the placement of an
interstock in a grafting process**
*Bilderback, Ted, and R.E. Bir, and
T.G.Ranney. "Grafting and Budding
Nursery Crop Plants". Published June 30,
2014, at NC State Extension Publications,
https://content.ces.ncsu.edu/
grafting-and-budding-nursery-crop-plants*

Spiritual authority is threefold. The first is the *Word of God,* the
second is the *Holy Spirit,* and the third is *Human Authorities.* Although
I had a revelation of who the third party was, the question of why
Ecclesiastes said that the *"threefold cord is not quickly [easily] broken"*
remained. I thought having the spiritual authority present as the third
party was enough but the Holy Spirit continued to reveal that **Connection Quantity** and **Connection Quality** determine if a threefold
cord is severed or not.

1. Connection Quantity

The level of synergic strength in a marriage depends on the **presence of all three forms** of spiritual authority, not just one or two. If
a marriage only depends on the Word of God but has no relationship

with the Holy Spirit and human authorities, they may stick together as a couple but when trying and challenging times come, they may fall victim to those challenges. The Word of God is like a paper road map. It will take you to your destiny if you know how to read it, but if you're not a good map reader (not understanding the Word of God at times) or face a situation that doesn't give you a clear answer like, "Should we move to this city as a family?" then you are bound to make several wrong turns.

A marriage held together by the Word of God and the Holy Spirit, although still not the best, is much stronger because it will have access to real-time directions. Like a GPS, the Holy Spirit provides us with real-time directions and what we refer to as "words in season." However, a person can still be prone to mistakes if they are unsure if the voice of the GPS guiding them is from the Holy Spirit or not.

Having all three is even better! When the above two are merged with human authority, it is like having a paper map, a GPS, and a tour guide present in your vehicle's terrain. Human authorities help to validate whether or not the directions you are getting are from the Holy Spirit, and also teach you how to avoid some of the mistakes or pitfalls they may have made or seen. They are also there to help us redeem time and prevent us from repeating negative history.

2. Connection Quality

It is not enough to have all three forms of spiritual authority present in a marriage, the **strength of their bond to spiritual authority** is a huge factor in determining if the threefold cord in that marriage would be broken or remain intact. The overall strength of the tree (marriage) is determined by the connection the husband and wife have with the Word of God, the Holy Spirit, and human authorities, both as individuals and combined as a couple. Just like a factory or plant line with several assembly stations, if one station malfunctions or is slowed down, it affects the entire assembly line and overall manufacturing time. Likewise, if there is a weak or non-existent connection of either or both husband and wife with the Word of God, the Holy Spirit, and human authorities, it affects the grafting process in their marriage as a whole.

This is the reason why when spiritual authority (the Word of God, the Holy Spirit, and human authority) is absent or loosely present in a marriage, there is a potential detachment between a husband and wife spiritually, mentally, emotionally, and physically. If their connection with spiritual authority remains loose, it has the potential of leading to separation.

Let's go into more detail about each party's responsibilities in fostering synergy in a marriage.

3

Personal Responsibilities for Synergy

"So again I say, each man must love his wife as he loves himself, and the wife must respect her husband." (Ephesians 5:33, NLT)

For a team to flourish and succeed in actualizing the vision and mission of the team, each individual must know, understand and fulfill the specific tasks and responsibilities assigned to them. This reminds me of a triangle (see Figure 2) with three points connected. Usually, you have one pivotal point at the top and two pivotal points at the bottom that are all connected, without any gap of entry, allowing the connection to remain intact. The top pivotal point is the spiritual authority (the Word of God, the Holy Spirit, and the human authority), and is higher than the other two points, while the two pivotal points at the bottom are the husband and the wife. You will notice that the bottom points in a typical triangle are on the same level but in different positions (which refers to the different roles in marriage).

Figure 2: Triangular Connection between Spiritual
Authorities, a Wife and a Husband

The husband and wife are individually responsible for building and developing their personal connection with spiritual authority. You'll see this demonstrated in the triangle with each of their pivotal points having their connection to the third and uppermost point. Any break or weakness in those connections will create a gap and a loophole/opening for external factors or parties to intrude. For example, in the early years of our marriage, I leaned more towards prioritizing our family devotions/connections with God than going deep into my personal relationship with God. While having a collective/group devotion is fantastic and aids with spiritually bonding together as a family, I came to realize that having my own personal and individual relationship with God through His Word, the Holy Spirit, and the human authorities God has placed in our lives, was also crucial in me building and developing my spiritual walk, which inadvertently helped us to bond as a couple as well. Synergy is all about team effort, but if part of the team is weak, then the whole team is also weak. A team's true strength is based on the strength level of the weakest link.

There are two categories of personal responsibilities in developing synergy in a marriage. These include:

1. **Connection with Spiritual Authorities**
2. **Connection with Your Spouse**

CONNECTION WITH SPIRITUAL AUTHORITIES

Both parties must take responsibility for cultivating their connection with the Word of God, the Holy Spirit, and the human spiritual authorities God has placed in their lives. This connection will eventually trickle down in binding the spouses together as one.

It goes beyond knowing or having spiritual authority in one's life, but also **submitting** to them. Submission is a deliberate and conscious decision to yield and be under the authority of another. In the context of marriage, this involves yielding and following the leading and direction of spiritual authorities (the Word, Holy Spirit, and human authorities) in one's life, even when we do not agree or feel like it.

RESPONSIBILITY 1:

Connect & Submit to the Word of God

"12 For the word of God is living and active and full of power [making it operative, energizing, and effective]. It is sharper than any two-edged [a]sword, penetrating as far as the division of the [b]soul and spirit [the completeness of a person], and of both joints and marrow [the deepest parts of our nature], exposing and judging the very thoughts and intentions of the heart." (Hebrews 4:12, AMP)

The Word of God is a powerful tool, that if yielded and submitted to, can influence every aspect of our being, including our spirit, soul (will, mind, emotions), and body. The Word of God is God's very words to you and provides us with wisdom for every aspect of life, including marriage. We are reminded in Proverbs 13:2 that he that walks with the wise shall be wise, and guess what? The surest and wisest to follow is the Word of God. It reveals depths of wisdom that surpass any earthly wisdom and shows you steps to take in developing and establishing synergy in your marriage. It is no wonder that Proverbs 14:1 shows the distinction between a wise woman and a foolish woman. One of the secrets of the wise woman in this scripture was spending time with the word of God and deriving godly principles from it.

"The wise woman builds her house [on a foundation of godly precepts, and her household thrives], But the foolish one [who lacks spiritual insight] tears it down with her own hands [by ignoring godly principles]." (Proverbs 14:1, Amplified)

The Word of God goes beyond just reading it daily but also requires meditating on it. Just like eating goes beyond putting food in your mouth, but also requires you to chew and swallow it to produce nutrients for your body; likewise, the same principles apply to the Word of God. It takes meditating on the Word of God with the help of the Holy Spirit and applying it to your life to begin to see the results from it. As you spend time in the Word of God, you will begin to see different wisdom strategies in handling different matters in your marriage.

RESPONSIBILITY 2:
Connect & Submit to the Holy Spirit

As mentioned previously, the Holy Spirit is like our real-time GPS. Someone once mentioned that the Holy Spirit is our **God's Positioning System**. I usually say I am a GPS lady because of how much I rely on it to move from one place to the other. So if we can all agree on how improved our driving is with GPS, how much more is the Holy Spirit being our guide? He is there to guide us into all truths (John 16:13) and help us navigate every aspect of our marriage.

I remember an incident in the earlier years of our marriage when myself and my husband had an "awkward moment" (misunderstanding), and I was so upset. My husband was heading out to work, and I remember the Holy Spirit telling me to iron his shirt. Honestly, that was the last thing I wanted to do, but because I was under the authority of the Holy Spirit, I followed His instruction (disclaimer: I did not "mistakenly" burn his shirt). I recall that the action I took left a huge positive impact on my husband, and years after that, he kept remembering the loving gesture I took, despite the awkward moment. The Holy Spirit knows you inside out and also knows your spouse. When we cultivate a deeper and more intimate relationship with Him, He will direct every step needed to solidify your marriage's fusion and synergy.

"But the Helper (Comforter, Advocate, Intercessor—Counselor, Strengthener, Standby), the Holy Spirit, whom the Father will send in My name [in My place, to represent Me and act on My behalf], He will teach you all things. And He will help you remember everything that I have told you." (John 14:26, AMP)

The Holy Spirit reminds us of what we have read in the Word of God and helps us in applying the truths from the Word of God.

RESPONSIBILITY 3:
Connect & Submit to Human Spiritual Authorities

Human spiritual authorities are the safety nets put in place, especially in marriage, to prevent us from falling into traps that can affect the synergy in a marriage. Have you ever heard some couples say how the first years of marriage were very difficult? One of the many reasons why marriages encounter such difficulties and suffer spiritual, emotional, mental, and physical loss is because of no active presence of human spiritual authorities in their marriage to guide them. Zipporah, Moses' wife, could have suffered the loss of her husband if not for the presence of Jethro, a human authority, who advised him to adjust his approach to ministry (Exodus 18).

My pastor once said, "The cost of being a human authority is more than the benefit a human authority derives from it." A true human authority is not interested in "controlling" your marriage as some people may think, but is there to ensure your marriage thrives and flourishes. Within the relationship of human spiritual authority, you can expect to be instructed by them, and receive directions and guidance on how to handle different aspects of your life and marriage. You can also find encouragement in them, especially when you feel like giving up on your marriage. You will be corrected on things that shouldn't have happened, and will also receive transparency from them about some mistakes they may have made and how to prevent such from happening in your home. Not everyone has been ordained to be your human spiritual authority. To learn more about who that person is, read the book, "*The Blessings of Being Under Spiritual Authority*" by Emmanuel Adewusi.

To get the best from human spiritual authorities, here are a few tips to keep in mind.

1. Be Open

Being open can seem vulnerable because you may be afraid that they will not be impressed with what they see. But that's a lie of the devil! Can you imagine a pregnant woman not willing to open up to the gynecologist during delivery because of the fear that they will not be impressed with what they see? The doctors are there to help her bring out the baby inside her, and the same applies to human authorities. Sometimes, couples do not see the life and greatness God has placed in their marriage union, and it takes the help of human authority that loves and has the best interest for you both, to help bring that greatness to life. Ruth was oblivious to the gift of favour upon her life, and even the moves Boaz was making towards her, but it took a human authority to give her direction on the steps to take (Ruth 3).

Open up about struggles or challenges you may have and they will be well informed on how to guide you through those. Hiding challenges from them does no one any good.

"Where there is no [wise, intelligent] guidance, the people fall [and go off course like a ship without a helm], But in the abundance of [wise and godly] counselors there is victory." (Proverbs 11:14, AMP)

2. Don't Put Up a Facade

Many people put up a facade before their human authority, intending to present this perfect image to impress them. It often stems from the fear of being rejected and not loved, but the truth is, there is nothing you can ever do to make another human being love you. Love is a choice and not something earned. Trust, however, is different from love and based on track records. You need to remember that the ordained human spiritual authorities God has placed in your life love you no matter what. Can you imagine a parent hating a baby because they pooped in their diapers? Don't try to buy their love, instead, just be yourself. If God has ordained them to be a human spiritual authority over you, the love would be mutual and not unrequited or withheld.

3. Listen to Them

Many times, in an attempt to try to impress a human spiritual authority, some people present all their good reports to them and do most of the speaking and very little listening. Many fall prey to just "hearing" with their ears but not actively "listening." One of the benefits derived from having human spiritual authority is in their words of wisdom. Sometimes, what they might be telling you might seem like a refresher of what you already know, but it might be one statement or approach they mention that will make a whole difference.

"Hear, O children, the instruction of a father, And pay attention [and be willing to learn] so that you may gain understanding and intelligent discernment." (Proverbs 4:1, AMP)

4. Ask Questions

"It is the glory of God to conceal a matter, But the glory of kings is to search out a matter." (Proverbs 25:2, NKJV)

One way we learn and grow in our understanding is by asking questions. An unasked question remains a possible area of ignorance. Ignorance is not bliss and opens the door to repeated mistakes and frustration. Asking the right question to the right person brings about clarity and direction. Human spiritual authorities are an avenue to increase our knowledge bank, which results in wisdom when applied.

5. Apply Their Teachings

Wisdom is the correct application of knowledge. It is not enough to take notes when spending time with your human spiritual authorities. True joy comes to a human authority when they see you applying principles they have mentioned during those sessions. Without application, results cannot be achieved.

"I have no greater joy than to hear that my children walk in truth." (3 John 1:4, NKJV)

Please keep in mind that their teachings are not just restricted to the conversations had in person or over the phone, but also extend to materials/books they have written and also observations of their life and actions. I have learned some amazing lessons from my spiritual parents just by observing them. No words were spoken, but their actions spoke volumes. Elisha saw Elijah divide the Jordan River by using the mantle. When Elijah was taken to heaven, facing the Jordan River, he did the very same thing he had observed Elijah do.

"8 Now Elijah took his mantle, rolled it up, and struck the water; and it was divided this way and that, so that the two of them crossed over on dry ground. 13 He also took up the mantle of Elijah that had fallen from him, and went back and stood by the bank of the Jordan. 14 Then he took the mantle of Elijah that had fallen from him, and struck the water, and said, "Where is the Lord God of Elijah?" And when he also had struck the water, it was divided this way and that; and Elisha crossed over." (2 Kings 2:8, 13-14, NKJV)

6. Love and Honour Them

According to the Cambridge Dictionary, honour is celebrating or showing great respect for someone or something. Honour is a virtue that draws out great treasures from human spiritual authority. True honour is a thing of the heart, that is expressed in the thought realm and eventually overflows into our speech and actions. There has to be a value you see and admire in your human spiritual authority before true honour can be activated. Someone once said: "you can't draw anything from someone you do not value." There are certain inspirations and revelations that God will release through a human spiritual authority, that can only be triggered by the catalyst of honour. This was a principle Esther walked with at different points in time. She always drew favour from those that have been placed over her. For example, Hegai was the eunuch over the women to be presented to King Xerxes during his selection of a new queen, but Esther impressed him so much that he went far beyond for her.

"Hegai was very impressed with Esther and treated her kindly. He quickly ordered a special menu for her and provided her with beauty treatments. He also assigned her seven maids specially chosen from the king's palace, and he moved her and her maids into the best place in the harem." (Esther 2:9, NLT)

This same principle of honour was triggered when Isaac asked Esau to make his favourite food to trigger a blessing over Esau. It is not because Rebecca couldn't cook the meal for Isaac, but Isaac wanted Esau to honour him so that he would release a blessing that could not be revoked.

"When Isaac was old and his eyes were dim so that he could not see, he called Esau his elder son, and said to him, My son! And he answered him, Here I am. 2 He said, See here now; I am old, I do not know when I may die.3 So now, I pray you, take your weapons, your [arrows in a] quiver and your bow, and go out into the open country and hunt game for me, 4 And prepare me appetizing meat, such as I love, and bring it to me, that I may eat of it, [preparatory] to giving you my blessing [as my firstborn] before I die." (Genesis 27:1-4, AMPC)

Honour is specific to a person, and not one size fits all. What might seem honourable to one person might be completely different and maybe even dishonourable to someone else. To display true honour, study and observe your human spiritual authority. Understand their honour language and operate with such understanding towards them.

True honour should not be done with a wrong motive but requires you to walk in love with your human spiritual authority.

Connecting with human spiritual authority is a heart-to-heart connection. It goes beyond words but heart-deep. One way you will know the connection with them is weak is that when you think of them, it's passive or you don't feel loved. This indicates that you have a weak connection and need to boost your connection. To strengthen a deeper connection and bond with human spiritual authorities, something of value needs to be going out from you to them regularly. Some practical steps in fostering a deeper connection with human spiritual authorities include:

a. Sending Them Appreciative or Encouraging Words - Make sure it isn't generic or something copied from the internet but something specific to them. Remind them of how much they have been a blessing to you.

b. Serving Them -This could be in specific areas where assistance or a hand is needed, and you extend an act of service to them. For example, if a human authority desires to write a book, assisting with transcribing one of their sermons into a book would be an act of service with a personal touch to them.

c. Giving -This could be in the form of monetary or non-monetary gifts for them. This shouldn't be always reserved for their birthdays or specific milestones in their lives, but even random gifts as a "pleasant surprise."

d. Praying for Them -We tend to bond with those we pray for and as instructed in 1 Timothy 2:2 to pray for authorities, this also includes human spiritual authorities.

A Word to Wives - Sometimes, some wives hide behind their husband's shadows and don't see the need to build deep roots with their human spiritual authority. It is important that you also have a personal relationship with them, as this provides an avenue for your specific needs as a wife to be met. Remember, in the triangular model, one pivotal point extends from the wife to spiritual authorities, and another pivotal point extends from the husband to spiritual authorities. Don't die behind the shadow of your husband!

CONNECTION WITH YOUR SPOUSE

The third connective line in the triangular model is from the pivotal point of the husband that runs towards the pivotal point of the wife. The connection that the spouses have to each other is very critical. It is not enough for both spouses to only be connected to spiritual authorities; as the connection they have for each other is also vital in producing a synergic effect in their marriage.

Let's look at some responsibilities spouses have to each other.

RESPONSIBILITY 1:

Know & Understand the Vision of Your Marriage

This is knowing why God has brought you together in marriage and what vision you are meant to achieve. If God ordained your marriage, it was because He had a vision in mind and saw you both as perfect candidates, fit for achieving His vision and purpose. Proverbs 29:18a tells us *"Where there is no vision, the people perish"* (KJV). Many marriages are in shambles today because they lack a clear vision. Terri Savelle Foy once said, "If the vision is clear, the results will appear." When vision is lacking, there would be a lack of direction, which eventually introduces frustration. Before marriage, this is something couples can do together prayerfully, to ensure their marriage is starting on the right foundation. However, if you didn't do this before marriage, it's not too late. Simply go to God in prayer to seek out what He intends for you both to achieve in and through your marriage. As the Holy Spirit gives revelation, write them out together and discuss. For example, part of God's vision for marriage is raising godly seeds, which goes far beyond just giving birth to children. It also includes raising them in a godly manner, equipped to expand God's bidding here on this earth. Raising children is not about just one generation but a bloodline. It is a bloodline and lineage affair!

"14 You cry out, "Why doesn't the Lord accept my worship?" I'll tell you why! Because the Lord witnessed the vows you and your wife made when you were young. But you have been unfaithful to her, though she remained your faithful partner, the wife of your marriage vows. 15 Didn't the Lord make you one with your wife? In body and spirit you are his[b] And what does he want? Godly children from your union. So guard your heart; remain loyal to the wife of your youth." (Malachi 2:14-15, NLT)

RESPONSIBILITY 2:
Know & Understand Your Place in Your Marriage

"And the Lord God took the man and put him in the Garden of Eden to tend and guard and keep it." (Genesis 2:15, AMPC)

When God created man (Adam), He gave him an assignment (responsibility) to tend, guard and keep the Garden of Eden. When you read the preceding verses, you will notice that the Garden of Eden was filled with valuable things in it, such as the Tree of Life and the Tree of Knowledge of Good and Evil. These trees were so valuable, that when Adam and Eve were driven out of the garden after they had sinned, two Cherubims with swords were placed there to guard it.

1. Adam's Responsibility

Adam's responsibility was to ensure that he did not eat the fruit of the tree of knowledge of good and evil, and since he was one with his wife, Eve, that inadvertently meant Eve was also not meant to eat from the tree. As a guardian/ custodian of the garden, he was meant to be aware of the state of the garden and any occurrences that took place in it.

Part of the responsibility of a guard is being aware that intruders' goal is to invade, steal and tamper with items of value that should be protected. Unfortunately, Adam failed in his assignment of guarding the garden against intruders, because the serpent (possessed by the devil) was able to enter and have a full-blown conversation with Eve while Adam was nowhere to be found. Even when Eve went to the tree, picked up the fruit, and ate, there was no indication in the scriptures that Adam was aware. But, even if he was aware, then it shows that he was very passive and instead ate the fruit offered to him from the forbidden tree.

"6 And when the woman saw that the tree was good (suitable, pleasant) for food and that it was delightful to look at, and a tree to be desired in order to make one wise, she took of its fruit and ate; and she gave some also to her husband, and he ate. 7 Then the eyes of them both were opened, and they knew that they were naked; and they sewed fig leaves together and made themselves apronlike girdles. 8 And they heard the sound of the Lord God walking in the garden in the cool of the day, and Adam and his wife hid themselves from the presence of the Lord God among the trees of the garden. 9 But the Lord God called to Adam and said to him, Where are you? 10 He said, I heard the sound of You [walking] in the garden, and I was afraid because I was naked; and I hid myself. 11 And He said, Who told you that you were naked? Have you eaten of the tree of which I commanded you that you should not eat?" (Genesis 3:6-11, AMPC)

When God came down to meet with them, and saw they were in hiding because they were naked, God asked Adam, not Eve, if they had eaten of the forbidden tree. This is why any marriage that fails is the responsibility of the husband, who has been assigned as the head of the wife and home. As John Maxwell says, "**Everything rises and falls on leadership.**" God assigned the husband to be the head of the wife and family and has given him the responsibility of leadership, which every husband has to be ready to assume. As a husband, you cannot afford to be oblivious to the state of your marriage and what is going on in your home. The husband's responsibilities include:

a. **The Spiritual State of Your Home** - This includes being the priest and one that stands in the forefront spiritually for your family, which includes praying and interceding for your family. Joshua decided that he and his family would serve the Lord (Genesis 24:15). Many have said a praying woman or wife is needed in marriage, which is true, but the sole responsibility does not lie on the wife. The brunt of that responsibility lies on the husband to ensure that the spiritual state of his home is on fire and not lukewarm nor cold.

b. **The Emotional State of Your Home** - Husbands are reminded in 1 Peter 3:7 to relate with their wives in an understanding and gentle manner to prevent their prayers from being unanswered. This includes incorporating respect, honour, and gentleness in your speech, actions, and conduct towards her.

"In the same way, you husbands, live with your wives in an understanding way [with great gentleness and tact, and with an intelligent regard for the marriage relationship], as with someone physically weaker, since she is a woman. Show her honor and respect as a fellow heir of the grace of life, so that your prayers will not be hindered or ineffective." (1 Peter 3:7, AMP)

As a husband, you also have the responsibility to **protect** your family, including your wife emotionally from yourself, extended family, and people around you. Protecting your wife is not limited to physical protection from harm but also protection from anything or anyone that can damage her emotionally. For example, if there are words you know can damage your wife's esteem, it is wise to refrain from using those words with her. There are some words my husband and I decided not to use again with each other because of the negative effect it could bring us. Ensure you pray over your wife and speak words of life and affirmations to her. After David brought the ark of God into the city of David, he headed home to bless his wife after blessing the people with some gifts.

"Then all the people departed, each to his house, and David returned [home] to bless his household." (1 Chronicles 16:43, AMP)

When dealing with an external family, you have to ensure that she is guarded emotionally from situations or circumstances that could negatively impact her emotionally, from your family and her own family. God has placed you as a shield over her.

c. The Physical State of Your Home - The husband has to ensure that his family is provided for, even if the wife decides not to work. This is why one of the three factors that shows a man is ready to get married is having a job (other factors are having a vision and being under spiritual authority). The reason is, having a job allows him to cater to his family's needs, which now becomes his new responsibility.

"If anyone fails to provide for his own, and especially for those of his own family, he has denied the faith [by disregarding its precepts] and is worse than an unbeliever [who fulfills his obligation in these matters]" (1 Timothy 5:8, AMP)

In addition to providing financially for the family, the husband is also responsible for protecting his family physically. Security is one of the responsibilities of a man. At the beginning of creation, Eve was brought out of the inside of Adam, meaning she was securely placed on the inside of Adam, away from harm. This is the reason why a husband is a covering over his wife and family.

2. Eve's Responsibility

When God looked at Adam and the responsibility He had given to him, He decided that Adam needed a helper that would assist him in achieving the assignment given to him. The work was too big for just one man, and he needed an assistant, who ended up being Eve.

"18 Now the Lord God said, **It is not good (sufficient, satisfactory) that the man should be alone; I will make him a helper (suitable, adapted, complementary) for him.** 19 And out of the ground the Lord God formed every [wild] beast and living creature of the field and every bird of the air and brought them to Adam to see what he would call them; and whatever Adam called every living creature, that was its name. 20 And Adam gave names to all the livestock and to the birds of the air and to every [wild] beast of the field; but for Adam there was not found a helper meet (suitable, adapted, complementary) for him. 21 And the Lord God caused a deep sleep to fall upon Adam; and while he slept, He took one of his ribs or a part of his side and closed up the [place with] flesh. 22 And the rib or part of his side which the Lord God had taken from the man He built up and made into a woman, and He brought her to the man. 23 **Then Adam said, This [creature] is now bone of my bones and flesh of my flesh; she shall be called Woman, because she was taken out of a man.** 24 Therefore a man shall leave his father and his mother and shall become united and cleave to his wife, and they shall become one flesh." (Genesis 2:18-24, AMPC)

A helper is an extra hand that makes a task lighter and better and assists in achieving the intended goal in a timely and stress-free manner. A helper assists with effectiveness (achieving the right goal) and efficiency (avoiding waste of time, energy, and resources while achieving the right goal). A helper is not designed to bring stress into a situation but instead, they eliminate any initial stress present before their arrival. Can you imagine needing to carry a piece of heavy furniture and seeking the help of a baby? Instead, that would introduce limitations, frustration, potential injury to the baby helper, and liability issues to the one who sought the help.

When the suitable helper is found, it would be obvious to the man that he received a good deal because he moves to greater heights of glory. This is the reason we are reminded in Proverbs 18:22 that *"He who finds a [true and faithful] wife finds a good thing And obtains favor and approval from the Lord"* (AMP). Wives, we are designed to be helpers to our husbands, to ensure he operates in a new and better dimension of favour because of the good treasure they find in us.

If I was, to sum up the responsibilities of a wife, it would be summed up as "**To Adapt**".

ADAPTABILITY

Many people are very familiar with the scripture in Ephesians 5:22 that says wives should submit to their own husbands but not many are familiar with **how** to do this.

"Wives, be subject (be submissive and adapt yourselves) to your own husbands as [a service] to the Lord." (Ephesians 5:22, AMPC)

Submission or respecting your husband is a function of adaptability. According to the Cambridge Dictionary, "to adapt" means to "change your ideas or behaviour to make them suitable for a new situation." Submission in marriage is very subjective because it varies from one marriage to the next. What might seem submissive to one husband might not be for another, which is why the bible clearly states that it is **to your own husband**. It takes understanding the language of submission to speak that language to your husband in the form of adaptability. To speak that language of submission, let's break down what it means to be adaptable to your husband and explore practical steps of adaptability.

"33 However, let each man of you [without exception] love his wife as [being in a sense] his very own self; and let the wife see that she respects and reverences her husband [that she notices him, regards him, honors him, prefers him, venerates, and esteems him; and that she defers to him, praises him, and loves and admires him exceedingly]." (Ephesians 5:33, AMPC)

PRACTICAL STEPS OF ADAPTATION TO YOUR HUSBAND

1. Notice and Admire Him

Whatever you pay attention to is what you will notice. If you pay attention to your husband's positive qualities, you will begin to notice those positive qualities in him and similarly his negative qualities. It is wise to deliberately pay attention to the great and wonderful details and qualities your husband possesses; even taking an extra step by writing this out as a reference point. I decided to write out the amazing qualities of my husband in an electronic note that I reference, to remind myself of the blessing God has given me. It is very easy for us as wives to forget those great qualities when we notice a tiny mistake or even take for granted some things they do for us because of their love for us.

Here are some examples of things you can use in taking note of the great qualities of your husband:

a. His Value System - E.g. his fear of and love for God, his respect for and being under spiritual authorities (the Word, Holy Spirit, and human authorities), his respect for his/your parents, his great work ethic, his integrity, etc.

b. Who He is - *E*.g. his honesty, hard-working nature, loving nature, diligence, self-control, commitment, down-to-earth nature, his playfulness, his touch for excellence, his forgiving nature, his caring nature, his approachability, his attention to detail, etc.

c. His Contributions in the Home - E.g. he helps with throwing the trash, helps with laundry, helps with ironing your clothes, helps with bathing the kids, tucks the kids to bed, cuts the grass, does home repairs, leads the family devotions, he assists with the dishes, his cooking, etc.

d. His Way of Thinking/ Decision-Making Process - *E*.g. his spontaneity, such as planning date nights, his gentleness in handling tough situations and people, his analytical and rational decision-making skills, how he spins challenging situations and puts a twist of fun/adventure to it, how he listens to your opinion when making decisions, etc.

e. His Physical Qualities - E.g. his sense of dressing, bodily/ physical features of his you like, his voice- how deep or how calming it is, his haircut, his smile, his laughter, his hugs, his kisses, how he strokes your back, etc.

f. Other Amazing Qualities - E.g. his jokes, how he relates with the kids, his encouragements and how soothing they are, how he takes initiative, how he provides for his family, his protectiveness over his family, his quest for knowledge, etc.

The above lists are not exhaustive but just serve as examples. As you begin to take note of the amazing qualities God has bestowed on your husband, a fresh admiration will begin to well up on the inside of you and a renewed appreciation will develop for him. This triggers honour and makes honouring him a lot easier. At the root of true honour lies admiration. This is one of the reasons why children tend to see their dads as Superman because they only focus on the amazing qualities of their dads, which encourages them not to disappoint their children. There was a way Queen Esther honoured her husband, King Xerxes, that the very banquet Queen Vashti was trying to host by herself, King Xerxes gladly made for Queen Esther without her asking for it (Esther 2:18). Remember, admiration is at the root of true honour.

2. Affirm and Appreciate Him

Inside every man, a child is wanting to be noticed and appreciated. As a wife, you have to be your husband's #1 fan. He needs to know, without a shadow of a doubt, that you prefer him above all other men. One of the great qualities of fans of celebrities is how they publicly show their admiration for them without any form of shame. Likewise, wives have to do the same. Admiration shouldn't just be internal but need to be vocalized. Affirm him when he does something you notice and love. For example, if you notice he washed the dishes or cooked, tell him how you appreciate his thoughtfulness and kind gesture (whether the food tastes nice or not). Whatever you thank God for multiplies, and the same applies to your hubby. Whatever you thank him for multiplies as well.

"There will be joy and songs of thanksgiving, and I will multiply my people, not diminish them; I will honor them, not despise them." (Jeremiah 30:19, NLT)

RESPONSIBILITY 3:

Understand the Love and Honour Language of Each Other

Everyone has a way they want to be loved and shown honour. It takes a deliberate and conscious effort to understand your spouse's love and honour language and relate to them in such a manner. This is all part of taking the time to understand your spouse, and you can do so by:

a. Observing Your Spouse - This entails observing what they respond to, how it affects them, or what emotions or reactions it triggers.

b. Asking Your Spouse - Sometimes, it is as simple as asking your spouse directly what makes them feel loved and honoured. This also helps you to get more clarity on why certain actions, words, etc, enact certain emotions or reactions. It also helps you deal with any misconceptions you might have concerning them.

c. Asking the Holy Spirit - The Holy Spirit is the Spirit of truth, and He understands every human being way more than they even understand themselves. He is the perfect source of accurate information about your spouse. Remember, He was there when they were created and formed. He can let you know what, when, and how to show love and honour to your spouse.

LOVE LANGUAGES

Let's dive deeper into the Love Language of Your Spouse. According to the book "5 Love Languages" by Gary Chapman, there are five different love languages that communicate love to different individuals.

1. Words of Affirmation

This includes words filled with love and grace, seasoned with salt that uplifts a person instead of bringing them down. According to Proverbs 18:21, we are reminded that *"death and life are in the power of the tongue and those who love it will eat its fruit"* (NKJV). There are words you can speak to your spouse that speak life into their very being, while some words take the life out of them. For example, words such as "You are beautiful/handsome, I'm blessed to have you in my life, thanks for being such a great support to me," etc. speak life and uplift them, especially if their love language is words of affirmation. On the flip side, damaging words such as "you're good for nothing," and "you're such a liability to me," belittle them and sap out their strength even if they want to do more. Words have the power to create and have the power to destroy. Words are so powerful that God Almighty used words in creating this universe that we see today. Be careful with the words that you speak to your spouse.

2. Quality Time

Time! Time! Time! This is one commodity we tend to say we don't have enough of, but the truth is, that we create time for the things we value the most. My husband has said that there are competing visions in life. What we decide to create time for truly shows how valuable it is to us, and the same applies to our spouses. Every time you create time, out of your busy schedule, you communicate to them that they are valuable to you. For a spouse whose primary love language is quality time, they feel loved when you give them your full attention while spending time with you. They may feel less important to you if you are distracted and pay more attention to what's happening on your phone, such as checking if a new text just came in, scrolling through feeds on social media handles, etc. If your spouse has quality time as their love language, they may want to engage in activities with you. The main aim is to be close to you and be around you. Encourage such activities, and this will fill up their love tank.

3. Acts of Service

Another way you communicate love to your spouse is by doing acts of service for them. This entails assisting with tasks that might lighten their current loads, whether they directly ask you for assistance or not. It adds icing to the cake when you do such tasks or offer a lending hand with joy, and it is not done grudgingly. For example, your spouse might be preparing for a work presentation, and even though they normally assist with packing the lunches for work/kids, you decide to take on their tasks, so they can focus on preparing for their work presentation. This act of kindness goes a long way and communicates to them that they are loved and that you value what is of concern to them. Sometimes it might be a huge act of kindness but a lot of times, it is the little acts of kindness that we excuse away that matter. Every day is an opportunity to express an act of kindness to your spouse.

4. Gifts

It is commonly known that when a person is celebrating an important milestone in their life, gifts often accompany it. If you think about why we do this, it is because we want to communicate to the other person that we join them in celebrating what matters to them and we do so because we love them. If your spouse's love language is receiving gifts, it is not the gift per se that matters, but the thought behind the gift. For example, if your spouse has been talking about a particular item of clothing in the mall that they saw and liked in the mall and one random day (it doesn't have to be on a special birthday or milestone) you got that item and presented it to them, that gift will go deep. Not because it was expensive, but because it shows that you thought about them and what was so dear to them. It shows that you were listening and paying attention to the details of their life. In our eyes, it might just be a gift but in your spouse's eye, it is saying, "I see and hear you love," and that communicates love to them.

5. Physical Touch

You may think it is a no-brainer for physical touch to be one of the love languages when speaking about couples, but for a spouse whose love language is physical touch, it may be required more than normal. It doesn't have to just include sexual intercourse but any form of contact with the body. This might entail giving them hugs (you may hear them say they are huggers), kissing them, holding their hands, giving them back strokes, leaning on your shoulder, laying their head on your lap, etc. All of these actions communicate that they are with someone they feel safe with and love.

Personal Observation: As you take the time to learn more about the 5 love languages by reading the book "*The 5 Love Languages: Secrets to Love that Lasts*" by Gary Chapman, and even doing the assessment test, one of the things I have personally observed is that even though your spouse might have a primary and secondary love language based on the assessment, in different seasons in life, that love language might evolve to a different one based on the need as of that time. For example, a wife's love language might be physical touch, but when she is heavily pregnant, she may still desire physical touch although might shift towards acts of service, as she leans more towards her husband assisting with tasks that may become challenging during pregnancy.

HONOUR LANGUAGES

It is possible to love a person but not understand how they prefer to be honoured. The Merriam Dictionary defines honour as "to regard or treat someone with admiration and respect." Honour can be grouped into two categories: **Inward** and **Outward** Honor.

Inward Honour

1. Honour in Thoughts

Honour begins from the heart, from a person's thoughts, and eventually spills outwardly into our speech and actions. It stems from the root of admiration- seeing something in that person you value and respect. As you ruminate over it, you will notice it will become easier to display honour to them outwardly. If you dishonour someone in your heart or thought, it would be very challenging to consistently honor them outwardly. Yes, a person can pretend to honour them outwardly, but it would be just a matter of time before they exhaust themselves and can no longer keep up with the act. How we think about a person greatly affects how we eventually treat and deal with them. If we think about our spouses in high regard, we will treat them with high regard, but if we despise them in our hearts, over time, we will despise them in our actions or speech. This was what happened with Michal, David's wife, who despised him in her heart and eventually spoke disrespectfully to him and lost the opportunity for him to bless her. She ended up as a barren woman with no transferable legacy. (2 Samuel 6:16-23)

In accordance with Philippians 4:8, we are to fix our thoughts on things that are true, honourable, right, pure, lovely, and admirable.

"And now, dear brothers and sisters, one final thing. Fix your thoughts on what is true, and honorable, and right, and pure, and lovely, and admirable. Think about things that are excellent and worthy of praise" (Philippians 4:8, NLT)

Naturally, the mind tends to focus and ruminate over negative things, but it takes the discipline of the mind to zoom in and meditate on God's truth about your spouse. The book, *"A Disciplined Life"* by Emmanuel Adewusi, is an excellent book to learn how to discipline the mind. Focusing on your spouse's lovely, admirable, and pure qualities would foster a new admiration for him/her in your heart. As previously mentioned, it's advisable to write out a list of wonderful qualities you love about your spouse that you can reference as much as you can. As you meditate over these wonderful qualities, your honour towards your spouse will grow and increase.

Outward Honour

1. Honour in Speech

There is great power in the words that we speak. Your words have the ability to kill or give life to your spouse.

"Your words are so powerful, that they will kill or give life, and the talkative person will reap the consequences." (Proverbs 18:21, TPT)

What, when, and how we speak to our spouse matters a lot, and can either damage or build them up.

WHAT - What we say to our spouses can encourage them, motivate them, cheer them up, or, on the flip side, bring discouragement, anger, or frustration to them. Job's wife was an example of a wife that advised him to curse God and die (Job 2:9). This advice lacked wisdom, was void of any care or concern for his well-being, and showed how much she disregarded God. Let the words that come out of our mouths be seasoned with salt, filled with grace (Colossians 4:6), and build up our spouses. Let our spouses trust that the words that come from our mouths are filled with wisdom and kindness (Proverbs 31:26).

"Do not use harmful words, but only helpful words, the kind that build up and provide what is needed, so that what you say will do good to those who hear you." (Ephesians 4:29, GNT)

WHEN - There is the right thing to say at the right time. Naomi advised Ruth to approach Boaz after he had eaten and drank (Ruth 3). Some things to note:

> **a. To the Wives** - Some deep discussions cannot be had with your spouse after a long day at work. Allow him to refresh himself and be in a cheerful state before engaging in such discussions. Queen Esther had a pressing situation, where the Jews, including herself, had heard of the order to be executed soon. She did not rush to mention it to her husband, King Xerxes, despite the urgency. Instead, she prepared two banquets for him and Haman, before presenting her case to him. Without hesitation, he favoured her and granted her request. She walked in wisdom on deciding the best time to present such a pressing matter to him.

> **b. To the Husbands** - Do not bring up sensitive issues around when your spouse is menstruating or ovulating, as

hormones might be in a heightened state. During those cycles, be sensitive to what might be happening with your wife. She might be hyperemotional/hypersensitive or hyper-cranky. Allow the wisdom of God to guide you on when you can discuss certain issues, to allow a more objective response from her and not the hormones talking. During such times, be very sensitive to her and treat her with gentleness and patience.

c. To the Couples - Some sensitive private matters should not be brought up publicly or for the world to hear. For example, you don't need to announce in public if your husband is having erection issues or what style your wife enjoys. These are private issues that your friends do not need to know.

HOW - It takes wisdom to know how to speak to your spouse. The Bible records that Abigail was married to a foolish man named Nabal, but despite his foolishness, she was able to live with him. Even when David decided to kill Nabal and his household because of how ruthlessly he acted towards David and his men, it was Abigail's wisdom in what she said and the approach she took towards appeasing David that saved the lives of her household. It is no wonder that when Nabal died, David did not waste any time marrying her. Abigail is known to be a woman of good understanding. Some things to note include:

a. Gentleness in Your Tone of Voice - The Bible says, *"A soft answer turns away wrath but a harsh word stirs up anger"* (Proverbs 15:1, NKJV). When emotions are heightened, it can be very easy for one's tone of voice to change and project anger and frustration as we speak to our spouses. But we must be very mindful of our tone of voice, especially when dealing with sensitive issues. We may not always notice it, but the moment your spouse pinpoints an undertone of anger or frustration in your voice, please make adjustments, as ignoring their observation may push your spouse to sense danger and build up their walls, which is not the best for effective communication. Let your words be filled with gentleness and peace.

b. Addressing Your Spouse with Respect - Never talk down on your spouse. Doing so damages their confidence and self-esteem. How you address your spouse will determine how others (including your children) will eventually address them as well. There is a common saying that charity begins at home. You can't pretend to address them well in public if you are not used to addressing them respectfully in the confines of your home. Eventually, it will spill outward in public. Some words are very derogatory or perhaps give such a feeling to your spouse (even if it isn't a disrespectful word) and should never be used when addressing your spouse. For example, there are some words, although not inherently negative, that my husband and I have agreed not to use when addressing each other because we noticed they don't make us feel respected. If we mistakenly do, we immediately apologize to each other.

c. Protecting Your Spouse in Speech - Never use jokes, insensitive, or cruel behaviour towards your spouse under the name of a joke. They might laugh, especially in public, because they don't want to make a scene but they might be hurting inwardly. When speaking about them to others, it should be from a positive light and not from a negative point of view. Since others do not have the benefit of seeing the full picture of your spouse, this is one way you can protect them. If most of the things they have heard of your spouse are from a negative light, you'll inadvertently paint a wrong picture of them. This does not mean you have to lie about your spouse, but if there is nothing good you feel you can say about them, then say nothing at all.

2. *Honour in Time*

When spending quality time with your spouse, several things portray that you honour them. Some of such include:

   a. Respecting their Time - When you honour a person, you will honour their time as well. Remember, time is a person's life, and respecting their time is a way to show you honour their life. If plans have been made at a certain time, showing up late without any heads-up is dishonourable. Sometimes, this happens when the appointment was not scheduled into your calendar. Putting it in your calendar or having a reminder honours your spouse by demonstrating that it is a priority to you. In the case where you can't make an appointment on time, give them a call or send a text ahead of time, explaining why and reassuring them it's important to you. Don't just show up and expect they will understand.

Part of honouring your spouse's time is also being mindful of how much time you spend engaging with friends outside the home. This does not mean you can't spend time with others, but to prevent your spouse from worrying about your well-being, you can't leave the house without letting your spouse know an estimated time of when you will be back home. It's not honourable to them if they stay awake without an idea when you will return because you are hanging out with friends. It's a courtesy to let them know, so they can plan accordingly without worrying.

When at an event together, you may notice your spouse is ready to head home and you might still want to engage a bit more with others. Let your spouse know you want to engage a bit more while being mindful of how much time you're spending with others to make sure they aren't waiting for a long time. If you love to communicate with others, it is possible to lose track of time. Deliberately keep track of time and your spouse while engaging with others to ensure a balance.

b. Paying Attention - When a person decides to create time to spend with you, it means they value you, and despite numerous priorities, they consider you a high priority to them. When spending time with your spouse, distractions have to be put aside, except you both have consented to have a window for some pressing items requiring your attention. It is not just your physical body that should be present; every aspect of you should be present when spending time with them. For example: listen, pay attention to what they are saying, notice the details, and engage with them through questions or comments. If you're doing activities together, pay attention and do not seem like you were forced into it.

3. Honour in Actions/Conduct

There is an adage that says, "Actions speak louder than words." It is one thing to say we honour our spouse, but another when our actions or conducts depict honour. Our words should always align with our actions — as that displays integrity and builds a foundation of trust.

Queen Vashti was asked by her husband, King Xerxes, to come to the royal banquet he was having for all his people, as he wanted to display her beauty to everyone, but she refused. Her action of refusal to the king's command aroused the king's anger and when he consulted with his wise advisers on how to deal with her action, they answered:

"...Vashti the queen has not only wronged the king but [also] all the officials (royal representatives) and all the peoples who are in all the provinces of King Ahasuerus. 17 For the queen's conduct will become known to all women, causing them to look on their husbands with contempt (disrespect), since they

will say, 'King Ahasuerus commanded Queen Vashti to be brought before him, but she did not come.' 18 This [very] day the ladies of Persia and Media who have heard of the queen's refusal will speak [in the same way] to all the king's officials, and there will be plenty of contempt and anger. 19 If it pleases the king, let a royal command be issued by him and let it be written in the laws of the Persians and Medes so that it cannot be repealed or modified, that Vashti is no longer to come before King Ahasuerus; and let the king give her royal position to another who is better and more worthy than she. 20 So when the king's great decree is proclaimed throughout his [extensive] kingdom, all women will give honor to their husbands, from the great to the insignificant." (Esther 1:16-20, AMP)

As a result of her conduct and the advice from the advisers, she was removed as the queen and replaced with Queen Esther. It is very easy for our actions/conduct to display a lack of honour, even if it was unintentional. Here are some things to keep in mind.

a. Non-Verbal Communications - Communication is not just verbal but also non-verbal. There are some mannerisms, body language, or gestures that display disrespect. It might be how you look at your spouse spitefully or even a sound made with your mouth that comes off as rude or belittling. It might not be a big deal to you, but it is to your spouse, and because you love them, it should be taken seriously. Be mindful of what those acts could be and consciously make a decision with the help of the Holy Spirit to put an end to them.

b. Joy while Serving - Acts of service should be done with joy and not grudgingly. It is not encouraging when a task is being done as if you were coerced. It is a sign of honour when it is done cheerfully. If they asked you for assistance with a task or you offered to help, it took them acknowledging that they needed help, which is humility. Naturally speaking, humans are prideful, but it means they subdued the temptation of pride to get assistance from you. Make it easy for them to continue to remain in humility by completing such tasks with joy and not with complaints or murmuring.

4. Honour in Gifting

I'm super excited about this because, if you know me, I like anything that has to do with the presentation of gifts, food, etc. Someone in the food industry once said, "You first eat with your eyes." This means the presentation of food matters a lot, even before eating the meal. This is why restaurants are so concerned with plating your meals in such a way that arouses excitement and entices you. They go to great lengths to ensure every plate is clean and picture-perfect.

Likewise, it is not just about giving the gift, the gift itself, or the thought behind it, but how it is presented is also important. The thought and gift itself might come from a place of love, but how it is presented shows honour. No one would feel honoured if a person gave them money that is roughly squeezed up in their hands. They may think to themselves, "I'm not a beggar, why are they giving me money this way?" Our presentation of gifts matters a lot. I'm not saying you have to go all wild with it, but let it look presentable and appealing to the eyes.

With gifts, honour goes ahead of the actual gift. It softens and prepares the heart to receive and accept the gift before it is even opened. If you are to give a gift to your spouse, nicely wrap it with wrapping paper or in a gift bag or box.

When handing a gift to your spouse, add a smile to it. Don't let it seem as if you were forced to do so. Even the Bible reminds us that God loves a cheerful giver (2 Corinthians 9:7). If writing out a card, do so when you are joyful. You know, it is possible to perceive love when reading a card, especially when it was written out when joyful. All of these matter in honouring your spouse.

5. Honour in Touch

Gentleness is key when touching your spouse. Be sensitive to how your touch affects them. Do not be too quick to discard their comments about your touch. For example, a husband might not realize that his grip is quite firm because of his strength and might be hurting his wife unintentionally and vice versa. Likewise, never aggressively touch your spouse or force your way on them, especially with sexual intercourse. Rape can happen in marriage when the spouse does not provide consent. Remember, rape is sexual intercourse that takes place when consent is not provided. Anything that can harm your spouse or seems disrespectful to them should be refrained from (including being domestic violent with them), to prevent your spouse from developing trauma from your touch.

On the flip side, it is honourable to your spouse when intimate touch is shared only between you two and not a third party. In our world, there are ungodly sexual practices such as threesomes, forced or consented swinging (exchanging your spouse with someone else for a time period), and other ungodly practices that do not communicate honour in touch to your spouse, and it is also not pleasing to God.

RESPONSIBILITY 4:
Complement Each Other

According to the Oxford Languages Dictionary, 'to complement' means to **"add to (something) in a way that enhances or improves it; make perfect."** When a man and a woman come together in marriage, they are meant to complement each other, leaving the other person in a better state than before. It might sound bizarre that husbands and wives compete with one another, but the truth is, it happens. One of the reasons why this happens is due to a disconnect in their bond or a lack of it. When the fusion of a couple hasn't taken place, they are still operating as individuals, and competition is likely to happen. Competition breeds division because they have not yet identified themselves as a team in a relay race. The success of one is the success of the other. The Bible says in Ecclesiastes 4:9-10:

"9. Two are better than one, Because they have a good reward for their labor. 10 For if they fall, one will lift up his companion. But woe to him who is alone when he falls, For he has no one to help him up." (NKJV)

In a relay race, the baton is passed along from person to person, all to achieve one prize as a team. It doesn't make sense if one of the runners decides to run on their own and neglects the other members. This would lead to the entire team being disqualified. When both persons know and understand that they are one, their union in marriage is solidified, which allows for a greater reward. The Bible says *"two are better than one"* (Ecclesiastes 4:9). One will chase a thousand but two, ten thousand (Deuteronomy 32:30). This is an exponential increase!!!

There are losses when couples work solo in marriage, as they have a much smaller result for their labour. It's one of the reasons why my favourite word is "synergy". As previously stated, synergy is defined by the Cambridge Dictionary as **"The combined power of a group of things when they are working together that is greater than the total power achieved by each working separately."**

Let's examine how to deal with competition in marriage.

a. Identify What You Each Bring to the Table - This doesn't have to be regarding finances only. These can be the unique skills and giftings with which the Lord has endowed you both. For example, the husband may be excellent at seeing the bigger picture — seeing the vision and direction for different projects in the home — while the wife excels at dealing with details and processes. This is a perfect combination because you need to have the blueprint of the project first to know what direction to go. When building a house, you need the architect to draw the vision of the type of home, the number of rooms, etc. Afterward, it is passed down to a foreman and other contractors to build out the details of the building plan/blueprint, which may include details for the foundation, framing, molding, dry-walling, electrical work, etc. They bring to life the vision. A vision without knowing the exact steps for execution would remain as a wish.

b. Identify How Your Giftings Work Hand in Hand to Achieve Your Unified Goal - My hubby once said that "revelation is when two pieces of information suddenly come together into one piece". Each piece of information or item might have stood alone, but the moment you see how they correlate, revelation is birthed. This is usually the "aha moment," when the light bulb comes on. You can identify the unique giftings that you both have, but without the help of the Holy Spirit to reveal how those two pieces can work together for a greater reward, it might remain a challenge to draw the correlation.

c. Subdue Competitive Thoughts and Suggestions - The Bible says in 2 Corinthians 10: 4-5 KJV:

" *4 For the weapons of our warfare are not carnal but mighty in God for pulling down strongholds, 5 casting down arguments and every high thing that exalts itself against the knowledge of God, bringing every thought into captivity to the obedience of Christ"* (KJV)

There would be suggestions, thoughts, and possibly images of why you are "better" than your spouse, or suggestions of how you are inferior to your partner; all of which lead to comparison and jealousy. The Bible says where there is envy and strife, there are all kinds of confusion and evil things (James 3:16). The moment these suggestions and images are entertained, division begins and competition sets in. We saw this unfold with Eve in the Garden of Eden. She entertained the devil's suggestions, and from there, it introduced blame and shame. Stand on the Word of God concerning unity in marriage and rebuke those suggestions and thoughts.

God has ordained husbands and wives to work as one team; if they do, they will enjoy great exploits. We see a glimpse of what can happen when there is the unity of a goal in the story of the Tower of Babel.

*"1 Now the whole earth had one language and one speech. 2 And it came to pass, as they journeyed from the east, that they found a plain in the land of Shinar, and they dwelt there. 3 Then they said to one another, "Come, let us make bricks and bake them thoroughly." They had brick for stone, and they had asphalt for mortar. 4 And they said, "Come, let us build ourselves a city, and a tower whose top is in the heavens; let us make a name for ourselves, lest we be scattered abroad over the face of the whole earth." **5 But the Lord came down to see the city and the tower which the sons of men had built. 6 And the Lord said, "Indeed the people are one and they all have one language, and this is what they begin to do; now nothing that they propose to do will be withheld from them.*** (Genesis 11: 1-6 NKJV)

God "**saw**" what they "**had built**," even though they were yet to build it physically. He knew their unity would have made them achieve it. The Trinity (God the Father, God the Son, and God, the Holy Spirit) are one, and when you examine the beauty of creation that exists because of their unity, it's just amazing. I pray that the unity within the Trinity will exist in our marriages in Jesus' name, amen!

RESPONSIBILITY 5:
Be Vulnerable With Each Other

"And they were both naked, the man and his wife, and were not ashamed." (Genesis 2:25, NKJV)

After God created woman (Eve) out of man (Adam) and presented her to Adam, he confirmed her as the bone of his bone and flesh of his flesh (Genesis 2:21-24). They were both naked in each other's presence and did not feel any form of shame. When I first came across this passage, I didn't truly understand this scripture until after I got married. You see, as humans, we are not normally keen to show our nakedness to the world, but when a man and a woman get married, that is meant to change. Nakedness is not just physical but also includes the emotional, mental, and spiritual aspects of a person's life. Let's look at some practical examples of what it means to be vulnerable in these different areas:

1. Physical Vulnerability

a. Body - Sometimes, spouses get into the habit of withholding sexual intercourse from their spouse as a form of punishment, or reserve it as a reward for something they desire. This is not acceptable biblically because your body is not your own. The Bible reminds us in 1 Corinthians 7:3-5 that husbands and wives are not to deny their spouse of sexual intimacy, except with mutual consent. This should only be for a period to prevent the other from falling into temptation.

"3 The husband should fulfill his wife's sexual needs, and the wife should fulfill her husband's needs. 4 The wife gives authority over her body to her husband, and the husband gives authority over his body to his wife. 5 Do not deprive each other of sexual relations, unless you both agree to refrain from sexual intimacy for a limited time so you can give yourselves more completely to prayer. Afterward, you should come together again so that Satan won't be able to tempt you because of your lack of self-control." (1 Corinthians 7:3-5, NLT)

b. Your True Look - Don't hide your true look from your spouse, whether it's your face, skin tone, weight, or hair. There is nothing wrong with enhancing those features, such as occasionally wearing makeup, wigs, etc, but when it is done to hide yourself because you are uncomfortable with your looks and as such, ashamed of your spouse seeing you in your natural state, vulnerability is not present. This underlying discomfort needs to be dealt with for true vulnerability to take place.

c. Health Status - Openness concerning your previous or current health status allows couples to come together as one in fighting against sickness or infirmities, not just for the affected spouse but also for your children and the future generation. As it's commonly said, prevention is better than cure, hence once your spouse knows of any hereditary health conditions, they can work together with you in ensuring preventive measures are taken, to prevent such patterns from being repeated in the next generation. E.g someone battling diabetes, would ensure their lifestyle and dietary choices are healthy to prevent diabetes in their children's health.

d. Finances - When you said, "With this ring, I thee wed and with all my worldly goods, I thee endow" as part of your wedding vows or a version of it, the "worldly goods" include your finances. Your spouse has the right to know ALL your financial abundance, commitments, and any debts. You can't start a building project or investment or have a different bank account and hide such information from them. This creates division and erodes trust in relationships.

2. Emotional Vulnerability

Emotions are natural reactions triggered by different occurrences in life, including experiences, moods, and relationships with others (Oxford Languages Dictionary). A crucial makeup of a person is their emotions. It makes us relatable to others as everyone experiences similar emotions. Hiding your emotions from your spouse is hiding a crucial aspect of yourself.

a. Outward Expressions of Emotions - When you are excited, express it to your spouse through facial expressions such as laughter, smiling, and grinning. This allows your spouse to understand situations or things that excite you. On the other hand, if a situation occurs that triggers tears, do not hide the tears. Some men have been taught that men do not cry, but this is a lie from the pit of hell. When Jesus' friend, Lazarus, died and He saw how people were crying, Jesus himself wept! Expressing tears is not a sign of weakness because a person is grieving or going through a challenging situation. Instead, it is a sign of a person being emotionally healthy and being able to express empathy, which is an expression of love.

"32 Then, when Mary came where Jesus was, and saw Him, she fell down at His feet, saying to Him, "Lord, if You had been here, my brother would not have died." 33 Therefore, when Jesus saw her weeping, and the Jews who came with her weeping, He groaned in the spirit and was troubled. 34 And He said, "Where have you laid him?" They said to Him, "Lord, come and see." 35 Jesus wept." (John 11:32-25, NKJV)

b. Communicating Your Feelings - There is nothing wrong with expressing how you feel to your spouse. Even Jesus expressed feelings of weariness to His disciples in the garden of Gethsemane. His time to be crucified was drawing near so He took three of His disciples there with Him to pray and revealed that He was exceedingly sorrowful, even unto death. What matters is how you handle that feeling. Jesus did not allow the feeling to overshadow his decision but instead went to pray to get to a place of peace.

"32 Then they came to a place which was named Gethsemane; and He said to His disciples, "Sit here while I pray." 33 And He took Peter, James, and John with Him, and He began to be troubled and deeply distressed. 34 Then He said to them, "My soul is exceedingly sorrowful, even to death. Stay here and watch." 35 He went a little farther, and fell on the ground, and prayed that if it were possible, the hour might pass from Him. 36 And He said, "Abba, Father, all things are possible for You. Take this cup away from Me; nevertheless, not what I will, but what You will." (Mark 14:32-26, NKJV)

Anger is another emotion that many people are afraid to express, though it remains in their hearts. Anger that is not dealt with will end up becoming resentment and bitterness. There is nothing wrong with expressing your anger but the Bible reminds us not to sin as a result of it (Ephesians 4:26). Jesus was angry with the way the house of God was treated and he expressed it, while still in control of his emotions.

"13 It was nearly time for the Jewish Passover celebration, so Jesus went to Jerusalem. 14 In the Temple area he saw merchants selling cattle, sheep, and doves for sacrifices; he also saw dealers at tables exchanging foreign money. 15 Jesus made a whip from some ropes and chased them all out of the Temple. He drove out the sheep and cattle, scattered the money changers' coins over the floor, and turned over their tables. 16 Then, going over to the people who sold doves, he told them, "Get these things out of here. Stop turning my Father's house into a marketplace!" (John 2:13-16, NLT)

When you are upset, acknowledge, and communicate why you are upset (what caused it and how that made you feel). Remember, when communicating this to your spouse, it is NOT about who your spouse is, but how that situation made you feel. For example, "What you said made me feel belittled" versus "You are so bad with words." The first statement focuses on how the action affected you as a person, while the second statement is an attack on the other person.

Your spouse has the right to see all the sides of you without faking the emotions you might be experiencing. However, remember that your emotions do not have to control you. You have control over your emotions! A wise person once said, **"Let wisdom precede emotions."**

3. Mental Vulnerability

a. Inspirations - Just like we have 'watch parties' where you allow friends and families to watch the same thing you're interested in, likewise, sharing books, people or messages, or activities that mentally stimulate you with your spouse allows them to access the world in your mind. It helps map out what inspires you and shows them how they can motivate you when needed. I've learned some amazing principles because of some documentaries my husband has shared with me, which I sometimes even use as analogies during my teaching sessions.

b. Systems - Part of knowing the makeup of a person is also knowing and understanding their value systems, beliefs, and principles they hold dearly in their heart. For example, if you value integrity, expressing that to your spouse will help them understand that being double-minded concerning a decision might not be appreciated because this communicates to them that their words and heart are not aligned. A discussion with your spouse may be necessary to express your principles, value system, and beliefs that matter to you.

4. Spiritual Vulnerability

a. Vision - When you receive a vision or assignment from God, this is something that you should share with your spouse after you've moved out of the initial stealth mode period. One of the strongest ways that couples bond is through spiritual bonding. God created marriage for man and woman to come together to fulfill His ordained vision. When visions are shared and accepted, it knits the hearts of the couples together as one. This is because you are running in the same direction God has ordained for each of you, which is a connection point for you both. One of the reasons the building of the Tower of Babel was successful before God interrupted it, was because they had one goal, language, and purpose. Sharing the vision with your spouse builds excitement in them, which is extra fuel needed to run with that vision. If one person gets tired or discouraged, the other person is there to lift them, which helps with the continuity of vision.

" 9 Two are better than one, Because they have a good reward for their labor. 10 For if they fall, one will lift up his companion. But woe to him who is alone when he falls, For he has no one to help him up. 11 Again, if two lie down together, they will keep warm; But how can one be warm alone? 12 Though one may be overpowered by another, two can withstand him. And a threefold cord is not quickly broken." (Ecclesiastes 4:9-12, NKJV)

b. Revelations - Revelations are so sweet and can easily make a person feel like they are "high in the Holy Ghost" because concealed information has now been revealed. It triggers an inner joy with an outward expression of rejoicing, laughing, or verbal expressions such as "Yesssss", "Thank You, Jesus," "This is so deep Lord" etc. When you receive an exciting revelation from the Holy Spirit, don't just keep it to yourself. It is said that joy shared is joy doubled, so allow your partner to experience the excitement with you by sharing what you received. This also tightens your bond because you are bringing them into your world. Similar to sharing a great deal happening in a store you like with whoever is willing to listen, likewise, share revelations with your spouse. This might even trigger a deeper conversation that can bring about further revelation. Revelation is sweet, and please ensure you share that sweetness with them!

c. Instructions - After receiving instructions from God, understanding it, and putting systems in place to obey, proceed to share such instructions with your spouse. Not only is this another form of accountability, but it also communicates to them that you value instructions from God. Adam was instructed not to eat from a specific tree in the garden, and when the devil tempted Eve, you will notice that she repeated the instruction, which means Adam communicated it to her (Genesis 2:16-17; Genesis 3:2-3).

A Word to the Spouse Being Told About the Instruction - If your spouse shares an instruction given to them by God, please join them in prayer to seek God's grace to fulfill that instruction for their obedience to be complete. Zipporah was aware of the command about circumcision, and when the angel was about to kill Moses after speaking with God, she was able to perform the circumcision, which spared the life of her husband. Support your spouse in ensuring they fulfill that instruction from God.

"24 Now it happened at the lodging place, that the Lord met Moses and sought to kill him [making him deathly ill because he had not circumcised one of his sons]. 25 [a]Then Zipporah took a flint knife and cut off the foreskin of her son and threw it at Moses' feet, and said, "Indeed you are a husband of blood to me!" 26 So He let Moses alone [to recover]. At that time Zipporah said, "You are a husband of blood"—because of the circumcision." (Exodus 4:24-26, AMP)

    d. Victories - Celebrating victories alone is not fun. Remember, your spouse is meant to be your #1 fan! In Romans 12:15, we are reminded to rejoice with those that rejoice and your victories are to be shared with your spouse. This is a joint victory. If you win, your spouse also wins, and vice versa!

RESPONSIBILITY 6:
Jealously Guard the Bond of Peace

One of the glues that binds a husband and wife is the Bond of Peace. Ephesians 4:3 says, *"Make every effort to keep yourselves united in the Spirit binding yourselves together with Peace."* (NLT)

Maintaining peace and unity will not come naturally, but it takes a deliberate effort to do so. Peace in a marriage is a glue that binds and fuses a couple as one. It also ensures that unity is not broken between spouses and does not allow a gap to occur in marriage. This ensures you are of one mind, one goal, and one vision. Going back to the story of the tower of Babel in Genesis 11, the people spoke one language and had one vision they pursued. When peace is lacking or attacked in a marriage, it is as if one spouse speaks English and the other speaks French. This makes it difficult for each person to understand the other, produces a division of purpose, and makes agreement challenging to achieve. The Bible says in Matthew 18:19, *"I also tell you this: If two of you agree here on earth concerning anything you ask, my Father in heaven will do it for you."* (NLT)

When there is disagreement, there is no unity of vision, therefore vision is halted. God targeted the principle of agreement, to stop the people's vision to build the Tower of Babel (Genesis 11). Although the tower had not yet been physically built, when He looked down and saw in the spiritual realm that it was already built, He knew that nothing could stop them from achieving it because of their unity and oneness. The only way God could halt their vision — because it was misaligned with His perfect will — was to cause them to speak different languages, resulting in miscommunication, which eventually halted the progress of their project.

Likewise, the devil uses the same principle to halt the vision of a marriage, by attacking the peace. He knows that once peace is lacking in a marriage, agreement cannot be obtained, which in turn, negatively affects the vision of that marriage. Remember, achieving God's ordained vision is the sole purpose of marriage. When vision is halted, it reduces the reason for a couple to remain together and can end the vision if the necessary steps are not taken to restore the peace. **When miscommunication happens and it affects the peace in your marriage,**

this is a demonic setup to halt the vision of your marriage. Resist it with every fibre of your being! I pray that anything disturbing the peace in your marriage will give way in Jesus' name, amen!

Let's examine some steps to take in maintaining or restoring the bond of peace in your marriage.

MAINTAINING THE BOND OF PEACE IN MARRIAGE

a. Identifying Intruders of Peace and Resisting Them - One way to jealously guard and keep the peace in your marriage is by first noticing intruders of peace and deciding to guard against them.

"Be eager and strive earnestly to guard and keep the harmony and oneness of [and produced by] the Spirit in the binding power of peace." (Ephesians 4:3, AMPC)

For example, some peace intruders can be in the form of words. Some words have the potential to stir up offence and should be avoided, to maintain the peace in your home. There are particular words my hubby and I have decided not to use because we noticed they send a wrong message to the other person, even if it is unintentional. Certain gestures and body language can also be peace intruders. Actions such as sighing and dismissive looks — especially when discussing sensitive topics — can send the wrong message and can communicate a lack of interest to your spouse. Do your best to identify the things that erode the peace in your home and quickly put an end to those behaviours.

b. Gentleness - Another way to maintain peace in your home is through gentleness — one of the fruits of the Holy Spirit. The

Bible tells us in Proverbs 15:1 that, *"a gentle answer deflects anger but harsh words make tempers flare."* There are times that the atmosphere could get tense because of the sensitivity of the matter at hand, but gentleness would allow the charged atmosphere to deflate. Proverbs again tells us about a wise woman who builds her home and that a foolish one tears it down with her hands (Proverbs 14:1). It takes wisdom not to allow emotions to run wild but instead, to allow wisdom to prevail over emotions. The virtue of gentleness is something that is very precious in the sight of God, and it is my prayer that the Holy Spirit will grant you the grace to allow the virtue of gentleness to flow in your marriage in Jesus' name, amen.

"but let it be [the inner beauty of] the hidden person of the heart, with the imperishable quality and unfading charm of a gentle and peaceful spirit, [one that is calm and self-controlled, not overanxious, but serene and spiritually mature] which is very precious in the sight of God." (1 Peter 3:4, AMP)

c. Forgiveness - Lastly, to guard and keep the peace in your home requires forgiveness. Remember that you are both humans being worked on by God, and as such, make deliberate allowance for some areas of improvement in your spouse. Choosing to forgive the other person's flaws would allow peace to reign in your marriage. This is a characteristic of love, and we see that depicted in Proverbs 17:9.

"He who covers and forgives an offense seeks love, But he who repeats or gossips about a matter separates intimate friends." (AMP)

RESPONSIBILITY 7:

Entrust Your Marriage Back to God

Any God-ordained marriage is an entrustment from God, where He is bringing a man and a woman together to fulfill His vision. Marriage is more than "I like you, you like me;" it goes deeper than that. God has found two people He can trust to fulfill His divine purpose. This is why God releases a special kind of favour when a man finds a wife, which is considered good in the sight of God.

"He who finds a wife finds a good thing, And obtains favor from the LORD." (Proverbs 18:22, NKJV)

God only gives good gifts, including the gift of marriage. It is a huge responsibility when He decides to entrust us with marriage and it is therefore wise to identify what He expects from us. 2 Timothy 1:12 lays out God's expectation on how to handle an entrustment from Him, including marriage.

"And this is why I am suffering as I do. Still I am not ashamed, for I know (perceive, have knowledge of, and am acquainted with) Him Whom I have believed (adhered to and trusted in and relied on), and I am [positively] persuaded that He is able to guard and keep that which has been entrusted to me and which I have committed [to Him] until that day." (2 Timothy 1:12, AMPC)

Marriage was the first institution established by God, and it is wise to commit it back to the one who established it (the manufacturer, God) and seek His guidance in navigating our marriages. Entrusting your marriage back to God is based on the principle of dedication. For ex- ample, when dedicating a child to God, this is acknowledging that God has given you a good gift, and you decide to dedicate that child back to Him to oversee the affairs of that child. Likewise, the same principle of dedication happens with marriage. However, to properly commit and hand over the wheels of our marriages to God, we first need to know Him, believe in Him, and trust in His guaranteed ability to keep and guard our marriages. Let's examine the process of dedicating our marriages back to God.

PROCESS OF DEDICATING OUR MARRIAGE TO GOD

1. To Know Him

If you are going on vacation and need to leave your home in the care of someone, would you be more comfortable with leaving it in the hands of your best friend or a mere acquaintance or stranger? Likewise, having confidence in Jesus Christ is rooted in having a true and personal relationship with Him and not just "knowing about" Him. We can vouch for a close friend because of closeness and traits or virtues we've seen in them over time and would give them access to valuable things such as our home. In the same way, having a real and genuine relationship with Jesus Christ means you have a personal experience with Him, knowing that you can vouch for Him any day. Let's take, for example, God is true to His word. Examining the promises God has made to you, and people you know or read about in the Bible. Notice how God remained true to His word and fulfilled His promises, and that will build your faith in God.

2. To Believe Him

Faith in God is like a planted seed — it needs to be watered to germinate and produce fruit. We are reminded in Romans 10:17 that faith comes by hearing and hearing by the Word of God. Every time we hear the Word of God, be it through the written Word, anointed sermons/messages, or testimonies, our faith in God grows. As we ruminate and meditate on the Word of God in the above forms, our faith gets solidified. It becomes real to us that we are trusting God for things He can do. For example, testimonies are God's resume of what He has done in the lives of others and your life. This encourages us that if He did it before, He can do it again!

3. To Trust in His Ability to Keep and Guard Our Marriage

Ruth experienced three different losses within a short period of time — her husband, father-in-law, and brother-in-law. You would have thought that after such a traumatic experience, she should have never trusted in God's ability to keep and guard any loved ones against death or harm. But she was willing to go with Naomi back to Judah and declared that Naomi's God will be her God. That truly is trust!

This reminds me of the kind of trust Shadrach, Meshach, and Abednego had in God. They decided to trust God even if God did not rescue them. However, God showed up for them enormously. Though thrown into the fire, He ensured they were not burnt, and they did not even smell of smoke. God was showing off his ability to protect and preserve. God said He will be our rear guard, meaning He will always watch our backs (Isaiah 52:12). A person cannot truly trust without first believing in the past track records of God keeping and guarding His own.

Like Ruth, you may have also been through different traumatic experiences in your past relationships, and now there is a fear that your God-ordained marriage may fail. But one of the attributes of God is His faithfulness. He is too faithful to fail! If He did it before, He will do it again! He promises to never sleep and never slumber (Psalms 121:4). Trust that when you hand your marriage over to Him, He obtains full custody of it and takes complete responsibility in ensuring that your marriage blossoms and is fully protected from any form of evil or harm (spiritually, physically, mentally and emotionally).

"And this is why I am suffering as I do. Still I am not ashamed, for I know (perceive, have knowledge of, and am acquainted with) Him Whom I have believed (adhered to and trusted in and relied on), and I am [positively] persuaded that He is able to guard and keep that which has been entrusted to me and which I have committed [to Him] until that day." (2 Timothy 1:12, AMPC)

God does not leave His people behind, but He watches over them and the affairs of their lives, including their marriages. Look at the Israelites, when Pharaoh decided to come after them, He ensured that they would see the Egyptians no more (Exodus 14:13). God promises in Psalm 121:5-8 to constantly watch over us and protect us (including our marriages) from any form of evil.

"5 Yahweh himself will watch over you; he's always at your side to shelter you safely in his presence.6 He's protecting you from all danger both day and night. 7 He will keep you from every form of evil or calamity as he continuously watches over you. 8 You will be guarded by God himself. You will be safe when you leave your home, and safely you will return. He will protect you now, and he'll protect you forevermore!" (Psalm 121:5-8, TPT)

Dare to trust in His ability to keep and guard your marriage against any harm!

4. Hand Over Our Marriages Back to God and Avoid Taking It Back From Him

It will be dangerous if a front-seat passenger in a car decides to take over the wheel of the vehicle while the driver is driving and keeps attempting to do so throughout the journey. This is how it is for many of us at different times in our marriages. We first dedicate it to God and allow Him to take the wheel, but at certain times, we take over the wheel and begin to navigate our marriages based on our emotions, experiences, and fears. God tells us in Revelation 3:20, *"Behold, I stand at the door and knock. If anyone hears My voice and opens the door, I will come in to him and dine with him, and he with Me."*

The Holy Spirit is a perfect gentleman and would not fight over who has governance over your marriage. Committing it to God is a deliberate decision we have to make and stick by it, if we want God to take over our marriages completely. He has the perfect track record that shows He can be trusted, and whatever we commit into His hands, He can keep and guard it against any form of evil. He promises in Isaiah 52:12 that He will go before us and will be our rear guard.

This is one of my favourite verses because it means we do not need to keep watching our backs. God has decided to take that burden upon Himself. Hannah decided to dedicate Samuel to God and allowed God Himself to raise him. When we do likewise with our marriages, He ensures that it becomes exactly what He has ordained them to be. Align your will to God's plan for your marriage and watch it succeed as promised in Proverbs 16:3.

"Commit your works to the Lord [submit and trust them to Him], And your plans will succeed [if you respond to His will and guidance]." (Proverbs 16:3, AMP)

4

Benefits of Synergy

"9 Two are better than one, because they have a good [more satisfying] reward for their labor; 10 For if they fall, the one will lift up his fellow. But woe to him who is alone when he falls and has not another to lift him up! 11 Again, if two lie down together, then they have warmth; but how can one be warm alone? 12 And though a man might prevail against him who is alone, two will withstand him. A threefold cord is not quickly broken." (Ecclesiastes 4:9-12, AMPC)

You may be wondering, 'Okay, we have examined the different responsibilities for synergy, but what is in it for me?' The benefits of synergy outweigh the price to pay for synergy. If I were to sum up the benefits of synergy, into one statement, it would be "**A Good and More Satisfying Return on Investment.**" As a common saying goes, "There is no free lunch in life." Nothing good just appears but entails some form of responsibility and investment to obtain the best in life. If a person is alone, they can still get some good return based on the amount of work and investment they are willing to make. However, the return is way more, when another person comes into the picture. Let's examine the different 'good and more satisfying returns on investment' resulting from synergy.

SYNERGY'S RETURNS ON INVESTMENT

1. Extra Help

"Two are better than one, because they have a good [more satisfying] reward for their labor;" (Ecclesiastes 4:9, AMPC)

The first part of this verse mentions that "two are better than one," and this is true because it follows the principle of multiplication. God understood this principle of multiplication when He looked at Man (Adam) and noticed the need for a helper in fulfilling the vision and assignment He gave to Adam. *"And the LORD God said, "It is not good that man should be alone; I will make him a helper comparable to him."* (Genesis 2:18, NKJV) Pastor Emmanuel Adewusi once said, "Until a person collaborates, they will remain small. Synergy helps to build something way bigger". It is way more powerful to build a network than to operate individually. There is indeed great power in numbers. God designed marriage to fulfill His ordained vision, and He sent you extra help in the form of your spouse to join you in pursuing and achieving that vision.

2. Exponential Increase

"How could one chase a thousand, And two put ten thousand to flight, Unless their Rock had sold them, And the LORD had surrendered them?" (Deuteronomy 32:30, NKJV)

I was so excited when I first came across this passage. You would have thought that two people would produce 2,000, but instead, they produced 10,000, which is ten times greater than what they would have produced alone. However, examining the passage might pose the question, "How could this be possible?" I also wondered about the secret to exponential increase until the Holy Spirit helped me discover that the answer was inside the question, "unless their Rock had sold them, and the Lord had surrendered them." This speaks of **Divine Favour**; the "extra help" a couple receives when they marry.

There is a level of favour a person cannot obtain until they are married. This is why the Bible says in Proverbs 18:22 that, *"He who finds a wife finds a good thing, And obtains favor from the LORD."* (NJKV). The key is finding the "wife" and not just "a woman." A wife is a woman of maturity (not just physically, but spiritually, mentally, and emotionally) that has been designed out of a man by God to fulfill His assignment. A level of favour is reserved for those married because of the assignment ahead of them.

My husband once mentioned how the Holy Spirit told him when he was single that there is a level he cannot get to until he is married. When favour from God comes into the picture of two people working together towards a common goal, an atomic bomb has been created. It moves them from the realm of addition to the realm of exponential increase. Favour makes things better and adds uncommon ease, making the journey and work extra sweet and enjoyable. It eliminates the toiling that is present without "Divine help."

"The blessing of the LORD, it maketh rich, and he addeth no sorrow with it." (Proverbs 10:22, KJV)

3. Upliftment and Lasting Acceleration

"10 For if they fall, the one will lift up his fellow. But woe to him who is alone when he falls and has not another to lift him up!" (Ecclesiastes 4:10, AMPC)

One of the sayings of the United States Marine is "No man left behind." This saying of theirs is based on the principle that each marine on the battleground must look out for the soldier next to them. After the initial excitement stage in the pursuit of a vision, there would be times when a person might be hit with discouragement, disappointment, and challenges of all sorts; which can potentially cause a person to lose sight of the vision or passion. When this happens, it takes another to encourage them back up through the grace channel of association. A person who is alone can strengthen themselves, but sometimes, it might be challenging to go through it alone. This is where grace through association comes in, and iron is then able to sharpen another iron.

"As iron sharpens iron, so a man sharpens the countenance of his friend." (Proverbs 27:17, NKJV)

Some challenges take the presence of your spouse to encourage you not to give up and speak life into you. We see this concept applied in cars, where another car boosts the battery of another car, for it to keep moving. Likewise, in marriage, upliftment from your spouse, whether spiritual, mental, emotional, or physical, recharges and boosts the downcast spouse back up on their feet. As this spouse gets back up again, like a wounded soldier that has another soldier carrying him, they can keep moving until they get to their final destination. Can you imagine how unfortunate it would be if a wounded soldier was all by themselves? Such a soldier might bleed out and eventually die. There is a saying that "If you want to go fast, go alone; if you want to go far, go together." There is great strength and momentum when we go together. This ensures that the vision is not halted but gains a lasting acceleration until it is achieved.

4. Warmth

"Again, if two lie down together, then they have warmth; but how can one be warm alone?" (Ecclesiastes 4:11, AMPC)

When two people lie next to each other, energy is created, resulting in warmth. Likewise, when a husband and wife are united and on the same page concerning the vision God has given them, it produces warmth in the form of joy, rejoicing, etc., allowing ideas to begin to flow. The Bible says with joy, you shall draw from the wells of salvation (Isaiah 12:3). There is such great power and strength generated when you know your spouse is rooting for you. Whether it is on a work project, business, or whatever assignment, when you have the full support of your spouse, there is so much strength that gets generated on the inside because you know you have someone on your side.

5. Reinforcement and Resistance to Attacks and Evil

"A person standing alone can be attacked and defeated, but two can stand back-to-back and conquer. Three are even better, for a triple-braided cord is not easily broken." (Ecclesiastes 4:12, NLT)

Anything of value to God will always be resisted by the devil because he hates anything that God loves. God loves marriages; hence, the reason it is the first institution created by Him in the beginning. As such, marriages are deeply hated by the devil, and he will try everything he can to destroy them. Synergy in marriage makes the couple aware that they have a common enemy (the devil), and their synergy allows them to form a fusion and alliance with God to resist the devil whenever he attacks. But what if a person is standing alone? In that case, there is an increased likelihood of being attacked and defeated because the enemy sees them as easy prey without any backup or defence system. Remember, if a couple is still operating as individuals and not as a united team, they are still "alone" and would only get the result of a lone person. However, when synergy is formed, you both are watching each other's back, and an even stronger fusion happens when the third person — spiritual authority (the Word of God, Holy Spirit, human authorities) — is present, making it extremely difficult for an enemy to prevail. This is the reason why a threefold cord is not quickly broken (Ecclesiastes 4:12).

The process of grafting is so interesting because when a plant is grafted to another, research says that the whole plant unit has better disease resistance than when they were single plants. Let's explore some ways we resist the devil in our marriage.

a. Through Prayer - One way we withstand the enemy is through prayer! *"Again I say to you that if two of you agree on earth concerning anything that they ask, it will be done for them by My Father in heaven."* (Matthew 18:19, NKJV) Prayer is a very powerful weapon in the hands of a believer. We see the impact of prayer in the lives of:

Jabez - He prayed for a change in his destiny, and God turned it from sorrowful to a destiny of enlarged coast and territory. (1 Chronicles 4:9-10)

Hannah - She, after being childless for a while, prayed to God at Shiloh. God remembered her prayer and blessed her with a son. (1 Samuel 1)

Isaac - He prayed to God for fruitfulness after noticing his wife Rebecca was barren. The Lord heard his prayer and Rebecca conceived twins. (Genesis 25:21)

Are you facing challenges in your marriage? It is not time to give up but to brace up in prayer. Isaac saw that the barrenness his parents faced in their marriage was now presenting itself in his marriage. He didn't decide to call it quits, but instead, he decided to fight against barrenness through prayer, and God heard him. When the enemy comes against your marriage in whatever form, let the Spirit of God in you raise a standard against him.

One of the ways a standard is raised against the enemy is when we pray in the Spirit or in our understanding. Prayer enables us to enlist heavenly backup against the schemes of the devil. It also allows us to bind whatever needs to be restricted or loosen whatever has been in captivity concerning our marriage (Matthew 18:18). Especially when we pray in the Spirit, this is a heavenly language that is encrypted, which the devil does not understand and this allows us to communicate with the Holy Spirit, thereby putting the devil in confusion.

There are times when you might perceive that something is "off" in your marriage, without the ability to pinpoint what the root cause is. At such times, praying in the Spirit allows the Holy Spirit to intervene and reveal what the issue is, for you to effectively wage war against the devil's manipulation. This is why the devil attempts to trick us by tempting us to not be in agreement with our spouse. Resist this temptation and foster unity and agreement by all means.

b. Through Wisdom - Another form of reinforcement comes through wisdom. We saw in 1 Samuel how Abigail applied wisdom in her actions and speech to save the life of her husband Nabal and those in her household from the wrath of

David. While Nabal's shepherds were in the wilderness, David and his men protected them from harm and ensured nothing was stolen from them. After this, when David heard Nabal was shearing his sheep, they asked Nabal to show them kindness by extending some provisions to them, but instead, Nabal ruthlessly insulted them. When word came to David, he became angry and summoned 400 of his men to kill Nabal and his household. However, Abigail — who served as extra reinforcement for Nabal through her wise actions/speech— hurriedly took gifts for David and his men and spoke wisely to David, whose anger subsided. It is no wonder that when Nabal died of a stroke, David married Abigail without any delay (1 Samuel 25).

c. Through Obedience - We can also overcome resistance when we walk in obedience. Zipporah was another example of reinforcement in preserving the life of Moses when he was going to be killed by God because he had not circumcised one of his sons. Her weapon in resisting this act was wisdom through speedy obedience to God's instruction.

" 24 Along the way at a [resting-] place, the Lord met [Moses] and sought to kill him [made him acutely and almost fatally ill]. 25 [Now apparently he had [b]failed to circumcise one of his sons, his wife being opposed to it; but seeing his life in such danger] Zipporah took a flint knife and cut off the foreskin of her son and cast it to touch [Moses'] feet, and said, Surely a husband of blood you are to me! 26 When He let [Moses] alone [to recover], Zipporah said, A husband of blood are you because of the circumcision." (Exodus 4:24-26, AMPC)

Moses' life could have been cut short before he even began his ministry, as a deliverer to the house of Israel, if Zipporah was not aware of God's command about circumcision, nor sensitive enough to discern that God himself was resisting Moses.

5

Hindrances to Synergy

"Do not be unequally yoked with unbelievers [do not make mismated alliances with them or come under a different yoke with them, inconsistent with your faith]. For what partnership have right living and right standing with God with iniquity and lawlessness? Or how can light have fellowship with darkness?" (2 Corinthians 6:14, AMPC)

God's design/ plan from the beginning of creation is for a man and a woman to be fused in marriage and produce a synergic outcome as they pursue His ordained vision. However, some factors can hinder or hamper the synergy meant to be produced in marriage. Join me as we explore what those synergy hindrances are.

1. Incompatibility

According to the Oxford Languages Dictionary, incompatibility means "the condition of two things being so different in nature as to be incapable of coexisting." Another definition is the "inability of two people to live together harmoniously." A man and a woman might be incompatible for several reasons, making it challenging for synergy to be produced if they get married. Some reasons for this include:

a. Being Unequally Yoked - In 2 Corinthians 6:14, we are reminded not to be unequally yoked with unbelievers, and this is because a believer and an unbeliever are of two different faiths. One's allegiance has been sworn to Jesus Christ while the other person's allegiance is to another god. Hence, this makes spiritual communication difficult, because their belief and authority have been given to two separate Gods, leading them in two completely different directions.

"14 Don't team up with those who are unbelievers. How can righteousness be a partner with wickedness? How can light live with darkness? 15 What harmony can there be between Christ and the devil[d]? How can a believer be a partner with an unbeliever?" (2 Corinthians 6:14-15, NLT)

b. Lack of Spiritual Authority - Earlier, we talked about the interstock or intermediate stock, a piece of a tree trunk inserted between a rootstock and a scion, to foster unity between incompatible varieties (Merriam Webster Dictionary; Ted, Bilderback, et al.). Where the two pieces are incompatible due to their differences, the interstock steps in to create a common ground and understanding between the two pieces, allowing them to fuse. Likewise, the interstock represents spiritual authorities (the Word of God, the Holy Spirit, and human spiritual authorities) in marriage. No two human beings are the same, and since we all have differences, friction is bound to happen when there is nothing or no one to properly manage and navigate the differences. Sometimes, one person may find it challenging to adapt to the other person or maybe even both to each other and require wisdom and advice from spiritual authority to understand and learn how to adapt and bring about synergy in their marriage.

The Word of God is there to bring about conviction and correction, allowing the fruit of the Holy Spirit to grow in us. The Holy Spirit functions as our real-time guide in providing wisdom and understanding of our spouse. Since He was there when God was creating them, He is the best resource for this information. A human spiritual authority, with the help of the Holy Spirit, is a safety net to ensure realignment if either party is misaligned and they also provide wisdom on potential pitfalls to avoid as you navigate the journey of marriage.

Based on the role each form of spiritual authority plays, we can see how important it is to have all three and not just one or two of the forms of spiritual authority, to avoid gaps. If any of the three spiritual authorities are missing, it loosens the bond a couple might have with each other, making it easy for external and internal intruders to infiltrate their fusion. For example, if a couple has a misunderstanding with each other and is tempted to say harsh words, they could refrain from that temptation because of their submission to the Word of God that says in Proverbs 15:1, *"A soft answer turns away wrath, but a harsh word stirs up anger."* (NKJV)

The Holy Spirit can then provide the right words to say to deflate the tense atmosphere, while the human spiritual authority can assist them in identifying the root cause of what started the misunderstanding. It's not to say that everything will always be rosy and void of temptation because you are under spiritual authority. However, the presence of spiritual authorities in a marriage gives the tools and grace needed to face and handle temptations and little foxes that can spoil the vine of marriage. Spiritual authorities help to deal with any unwillingness to adapt or a lack of knowledge on how to adapt to one's spouse.

2. Timing

Timing is an important factor in the grafting process because plants fuse over a period of time — it's not an immediate occurrence.

According to Ted Bilderback et al., the rootstock and scion must be prepared separately before the scion is inserted, followed by securing the graft with a graft twine, wax, or paint. Once all these steps are completed, the graft can now begin to successfully fuse. Likewise, before marriage, there are some steps of preparation that God, if allowed, takes an individual through in preparing them for marriage. Preparation would include things such as: dealing with wounds or past trauma, correcting some wrong mindsets or misconceptions, adjusting unrealistic expectations, and correcting character flaws, all to get them ready for the next stage of fusion in marriage. Unfortunately, not everyone is willing to undergo God's preparation stage and therefore hastily and prematurely run into marriage.

Marriage is not for boys and girls but for those mature — not just in age, but spiritually, mentally, emotionally, and physically. A couple that is mature in age, but not yet mature mentally, emotionally, or spiritually easily gives up when faced with responsibilities and challenges that come with marriage. For example, an individual that has been traumatized, especially in a relationship, is not ready for another relationship or marriage until they have dealt with it and healed from it. Even if the person they want to get married to is God's perfect will for their life, if they marry prematurely, the foundation is already faulty and shaky, risking such marriage caving in when (not if) the storms that affect any marriage show up.

" 24 So everyone who hears these words of Mine and acts upon them [obeying them] will be like a [a]sensible (prudent, practical, wise) man who built his house upon the rock. 25 And the rain fell and the floods came and the winds blew and beat against that house; yet it did not fall, because it had been founded on the rock. 26 And everyone who hears these words of Mine and does not do them will be like a stupid (foolish) man who built his house upon the sand. 27 And the rain fell and the floods came and the winds blew and *beat against that house, and it fell—and great and complete was the fall of it."* (Matthew 7:24-27, AMPC)

It takes wisdom (applied knowledge) from the three spiritual authorities for an individual to be ready to take the next step into marriage. As this knowledge is applied and they venture into marriage, they acquire an understanding of their self, spouse, vision for marriage, and responsibilities associated with marriage that produces lasting synergy. Understanding helps to replicate results.

"3 Through skillful and godly Wisdom is a house (a life, a home, a family) built, and by understanding it is established [on a sound and good foundation], 4 And by knowledge shall its chambers [of every area] be filled with all precious and pleasant riches." (Proverbs 24:3-4, AMPC)

3. *Competition*

God did not design marriage to **compete** with your spouse but to **complement** each other as you work towards a common goal. Division is simply having two visions (di-vision) and when this — di-vision — occurs, synergy cannot take place. This is because each spouse is working as an individual and competing against the other, which causes a drastic reduction in their final result. Remember, one will chase a thousand but two, ten thousand (Deuteronomy 32:30).

When di-vision is present, couples are robbed of an exponential increase. They remain in the realm of addition (just 2,000 worth) as compared to the realm of exponential multiplication (10,000 worth). When thoughts of seeing your spouse as an opponent come, resist them with every fibre of your being. This is a setup to steal from you (steal your exponential increase, leaving you with little reward for your labour).

Queen Vashti is an example of a woman in subtle competition with her husband. In Esther 1, we see that when her husband, King Xerxes, was holding a feast for the people all across Shushan, she was also holding her feast for the women in the royal house at the very same time. When the king requested her presence, she refused to come because of misplaced priority and unwillingness to adapt to her husband. She didn't see the feast he held as "their own feast" but just "his own feast," making her unconcerned about the outcome of the feast he held. This di-vision brought about a gap in their marriage, opening it up for intruders like Memucan to give the king the advice to remove Queen Vashti as queen, which the king followed. Whenever a competition is allowed to set in, the devil is given room in that marriage, and division is bound to happen.

4. Laziness

In Ecclesiastes 4:9, it says, *"two are better than one, because they have a good [more satisfying] reward for their labor."* (AMPC) Did you notice it mentions "labor" (or work) at the end? Nothing good ever comes without any form of input or work. Marriage requires work for it to succeed. A successful marriage doesn't just happen without both parties working towards it. Vision pursuit is at the core of marriage, and vision entails lots of work! It's like a baby that has been born and requires lots of attention, care, time, and investment to become who God has made them to be. My husband says, "An organization is born when the owner can no longer do the work alone." Likewise, when God created a wife, He did so to provide extra help to the man so they can achieve and expand the vision, making it into something bigger than what the man could have achieved alone. However, not every couple is willing to put in the work required to build a synergic marriage and when laziness sets in, decay is bound to happen. Any building that is not cared for, will eventually begin to decay.

"Because of laziness the building decays, And through idleness of hands the house leaks." (Ecclesiastes 10:18 NKJV)

Among the responsibilities required in producing a synergic marriage, as previously mentioned, one of the greatest works required from both parties is **Death to Self.** The selfish nature, which seeks only to please itself, needs to die before it can help release a harvest as a result of synergy. The "me, I" nature has to go, to give way to "we, us." This is why we are reminded in John 12:24 that:

"Let me make this clear: A single grain of wheat will never be more than a single grain of wheat unless it drops into the ground and dies. Because then it sprouts and produces a great harvest of wheat—all because one grain died." (TPT)

Epilogue

Myles Munroe once said, "When purpose is not known, abuse is inevitable." The purpose or essence of marriage is to establish synergy in achieving God's vision and will, which I have attempted to provide some directions on how to navigate, in this book. However, running ahead without God's grace will lead to much toiling and frustration. Tap into the grace that flows from the throne of God as you work in partnership with your spouse and spiritual authorities (the Word, Holy Spirit, and human authorities), and you will see and taste the synergic fruits God desires for your marriage.

Remember, synergy is not instant but a gradual process, so be patient with yourself and your spouse, and do not be weary. In due season, as you apply these principles, you will reap the harvest of your labour, if you do not give up.

Marriage is such a beautiful thing; God desires to beautify your marriage and make you enjoy the sweetness that lies inside it. I pray that your marriage will flourish and blossom into all God has designed it to be from the beginning of creation, and your marriage will enjoy the heavenly sweetness that has been specially designed for marriage in Jesus' name, amen!

A Sinner's Prayer

I will be delighted to lead you in receiving Jesus Christ as your personal Lord and Saviour. If you would like to take this fabulous step today, please say this prayer with me:

"Lord Jesus Christ, I believe You are the Son of God, and I believe You died for me on the cross of Calvary. I know I am a sinner, and today, I come to You to forgive me of all my sins and to make me a new creation. I accept You as my personal Lord and Saviour. Thank you, Jesus, for forgiving me and making me born again, in Jesus' name, amen."

Name & Signature _____

Date _____

Congratulations!!! You are now born-again! This means you have been engrafted into the kingdom and family of Jesus Christ. Truly, your life will not remain the same. If you made this decision today, I would love to hear from you and provide resources for your new journey! Please kindly visit www.cccghq.org/saved or share your testimony with me at ibukun.adewusi@cccghq.org.

Contact the Author

Thank you for taking the time to read this book. I'm positive you were blessed by it. I would be delighted to hear your testimonies on the impact it has had on your life and those around you.

To reach me, please contact me through email at ibukun.adewusi@cc-cghq.org.

Jesus bless you!

About the Author

Ibukun Adewusi, alongside her husband, Emmanuel Adewusi, are the founding and lead pastors of Cornerstone Christian Church of God. Together, they have been called to "bring restoration and transformation to all by teaching, preaching, and demonstrating the gospel of Jesus Christ."

She adores the mandate she has received in 'bringing restoration and transformation to families', which she believes is the bedrock of any nation. Through her blog, 'The Golden Nuggets,' she aspires to see families blossom, flourish and fulfill the vision God intended for them since the beginning of creation.

Ibukun Adewusi is joyfully married to her lovely husband, Emmanuel Adewusi, and together, they are building a thriving Christ-centered family.

Additional References

1.   Bilderback, Ted, et al. "Grafting and Budding Nursery Crop Plants." NC State Extension Publications, 30 June 2014, https://content.ces.ncsu.edu/grafting-and-budding-nursery-crop-plants

2.   "Graft." Encyclopædia Britannica, Encyclopædia Britannica, Inc., https://www.britannica.com/topic/graft

3.   "Interstock." Merriam-Webster.com, Merriam-Webster, https://www.merriam-webster.com/dictionary/interstock"

4.   "Incompatible." Cambridge Dictionary, Cambridge University Press, https://dictionary.cambridge.org/dictionary/english/incompatible

5.   "Synergy." Cambridge Dictionary, Cambridge University Press, https://dictionary.cambridge.org/dictionary/english/synerg

6.   "Incompatibility." Oxford Languages Dictionary, Oxford University Press, https://languages.oup.com/

7.   "Emotions." Oxford Languages Dictionary, Oxford University Press, https://languages.oup.com/

8. "To Complement." Oxford Languages Dictionary, Oxford University Press, https://languages.oup.com/ Lewis, C.S. The Four Loves. Mariner Books, 2017

9. Chapman, Gary. The 5 Love Languages: Secrets to Love That Lasts. The Northfield Publishing, 2009

10. Adewusi, Emmanuel. The Blessings of Being Under Spiritual Authority. 2017

Printed in the USA
CPSIA information can be obtained
at www.ICGtesting.com
LVHW020731021123
762684LV00006B/229

9 781989 099247